THE
GOURMET'S
LEXICON

Acknowledgements

Two people in particular are owed my thanks
for their continuing inspiration and
encouragement. **Richard Olney,** the force
behind Time-Life's cookery series,
possesses a keen palate and a hand equally
skilled with a pen or a wooden spoon.
Richard taught me that a love of good food
can be an integral part of one's daily life.
Elizabeth Lambert Ortiz, the author
of several fine cookery books, inspires me
with her enthusiasm for whatever is
new and exciting in the world of fine cuisine.

I would also like to thank **Alice Bandy** and
Michael Friedman for suggesting
that I write the book, and **John Smallwood**
for proposing it. Special thanks are due to
Bill Logan for being a tactful and skillful editor.

THE GOURMET'S LEXICON

NORMAN KOLPAS

A PERIGEE BOOK

Perigee Books
are published by
G.P. Putnam's Sons
200 Madison Avenue
New York, New York 10016

Library of Congress Cataloging in Publication Data
Kolpas, Norman
    The gourmet's lexicon.
    1. Food—Dictionaries. 2. Cookery,
International—Dictionaries. I. Title.
TX349.S96   641'.03'21 82-5242
ISBN 0-399-50674-8   AACR2

The Gourmet's Lexicon
was produced and prepared by
Quarto Marketing Ltd.
212 Fifth Avenue
New York, N.Y. 10010

Editor: Bill Logan
Cover Design: Ken Diamond
Text Design: Betsy Fox
Illustrations by Beatriz Vidal

Typesetting by BPE Graphics.
Printed and bound in the United States of America by
R.R. Donnelley & Sons.

First Perigee printing, 1982.

HOW TO USE THIS BOOK

Like any lexicon, this book's primary use is as an alphabetical reference. When, in your dining, you encounter some unfamiliar term, look it up: chances are, you will find it listed with a brief description of the dish in question and other relevant information.

You will find four main kinds of entry. Most numerous are those concerning styles of dishes—the *à la*'s of French cuisine and the *alla*'s of *la cucina Italiana* as well as various designations from the cookery of other lands. Then there are listings for specialties of the world's cuisines—keynote dishes that you will encounter on menus again and again, others less well known but worth seeking out and trying. Although this book does not give listings for ingredients, there are some broad categories of foods that while ingredients, are also dishes in their own right or so distinctive that they merit special attention: thus there are entries for FOIE GRAS, HAMS, HERRINGS, MUSHROOMS, PÂTÉ, ROES, TRUFFLES, WURSTS and more. Finally, you will find brief essays on the world's major cuisines, summarizing their characteristics and referring you to other entries about their finest dishes.

One kind of entry you will not find here is the simple translation. There are no listings that tell you, for example, that *boeuf* is French for beef or *pollo* Italian or Spanish for chicken. But look up *à la* BOURGUIGNONNE when you encounter it on a menu with *boeuf* or *alla* CACCIATORE with *pollo* and you will find a definition.

That said, I hope you don't just use this book as a pocket dictionary. All the entries have been written purposely not as terse definitions, but rather as brief discursive, sometimes anecdotal essays. And if you start with a major cuisine entry, you should be able to spend a pleasant idle hour, following cross-references through the book. Words printed in small capital letters within one entry have their own separate entry as well.

KEY TO ABBREVIATIONS

In each entry, the country of origin appears in parentheses following the name of the dish, preparation or ingredient. The abbreviations used are listed below:

AF	African
AU	Austrian
AUS	Australian
BNL	Belgium, Netherlands, Luxembourg
CARIB	Caribbean
EE	Eastern Europe
FR	French
GE	German
GR	Greek
IN	Indian
IR	Irish
IT	Italian
JA	Japanese
JE	Jewish
KO	Korean
LA	Latin American
ME	Middle Eastern
MEX	Mexican
RUS	Russian
SC	Scandinavian
SEA	Southeast Asian
SW	Swiss
UK	United Kingdom
US	United States

INTRODUCTION

During the past decade, nothing less than a revolution has happened in the way we eat. In our homes we have food processors that enable us to whip up a hollandaise sauce or knead a brioche dough in a matter of seconds, and microwave ovens that reduce cooking time, encouraging us to spend more time trying new dishes. In our search for recipes we buy cookbooks with a passion, and where once we read only our local newspaper's food column, today we may subscribe to any number of gourmet magazines.

Outside of the home, the revolution is just as active. The trend towards impersonal supermarkets and processed foods is being reversed by new, small food shops and farmers' markets which offer scores of cheeses and sausages, unusual and tempting vegetables and fruits, fresh pastas, home-baked breads, imported cooking oils and vinegars. New restaurants appear at an astonishing rate: some that celebrate fresh seasonal foods and regional specialties; others that offer their own interpretations of classic and *nouvelle* cuisines; still others where we can discover the best of the world's ethnic cooking. We plan gastronomic tours for our vacations. We avidly read and discuss food criticism and restaurant reviews.

In a small way, I have had the opportunity to become a part of this revolution. Accidentally launched into the world of cuisine by a few articles I did for *The Times* of London, I have since spent the better part of a decade writing and editing food books and magazines, from the Time-Life series, The Good Cook, to the journal *The Pleasures of Cooking*. Without ever having set out to become one, I found myself being called a gourmet!

I was proud of the name, but disturbed by the snobbery sometimes attached to it. When some people used the term, they seemed to imply that I had joined a privileged class, acquiring an expertise that few can hope to have. But I don't believe that I am privy to the secrets of some occult science or that gourmets constitute a secret society to which few are admitted. Of course, a love of food is essential to becoming a gourmet, and a discerning palate is an advantage. Otherwise, the key to being a gourmet is quite simple.

Words are the key. Any specialist—be it the lawyer with his torts and writs or the physicist with his quarks and neutrinos—is set apart by the words he or she understands. The gourmet too needs a basic vocabulary which will allow him or her to enter the world of fine dining with assurance. Gourmets can decipher a French or Italian menu. They are familiar with the names of wild mushrooms, of the choicest grades of caviar. Even if they've never eaten *sushi*, they have an idea of the kind of thing it is and will not be intimidated the first time they encounter it. Once the basic vocabulary is learned, they look upon each new dish's name with pleasurable anticipation instead of unease.

Through my brief career, I have often referred to the weighty reference works about food, trying to understand some new preparation or dish, but I always felt the lack of a pocket dictionary which would make up for in convenience what it might lack in encyclopedic comprehensiveness, introducing me to the world of fine dining without burying me in details.

That is why I have compiled this lexicon for gourmets and aspiring gourmets. In one handy book, you will find a cross-section—select and idiosyncratic, but representative—of terms that are important, interesting and sometimes amusing. It will help you develop familiarity with the world of cusine. Take this book as a foundation on which to build your own future as a gourmet.

O ye gods, what pleasure I have denied myself by being overfastidious in my tastes!

—ARTAXERXES,
KING OF PERSIA

ACHAR (SEA)

Indonesian for "salad," but a salad in the Spice Islands is a far cry from its Western cousins. In the standard versions, one or several raw or cooked vegetables—cabbage, onions, carrots, cucumbers, sweet peppers, string beans and potatoes are popular—are tossed with white or cider vinegar, sugar, salt and ginger; sometimes garlic is added. The vegetables are left to steep in the dressing for several hours, becoming lightly pickled. A Sumatran variation utilizes a cold peanut-butter sauce, a variation on the complex theme of the salad called GADO GADO.

ADOBO (SEA)

The national dish of the Philippines, it is a sharp-tasting pork or chicken stew flavored with vinegar, garlic, soy sauce and peppercorns. Depending on the part of the country in which it is prepared, it may instead feature beef or seafood or have the added smoothness of coconut milk.

AEMONO
See JAPANESE COOKING.

AGEMONO
See JAPANESE COOKING.

all' AGLIO E OLIO (IT)
This style of dressing spaghetti is hard to pronounce (AHL-AH-LEE-OH-LEE-OH is close enough) but well worth the effort to order. It is pasta for purists: just the noodles cooked *al* DENTE and bathed with hot olive oil in which an abundance of garlic has been fried, lending the oil its powerful perfume.

AGNOLOTTI
See PASTA.

AGRODOLCE (IT)
A savory-sweet sauce in which meats—particularly duck, hare or rabbit—or vegetables such as cabbage and zucchini are cooked. The savory elements come from red wine, olive oil, vinegar, chopped ham, onion and herbs; the sweet additions come from sugar or honey and such optional ingredients as candied lemon peel, white raisins, pine nuts and even bittersweet chocolate.

AÏOLI (FR)
Taking its name from the French *ail*, or garlic, this Provençal mayonnaise sauce is flavored with an abundance of crushed garlic cloves. It is excellent with hot or cold poached fish, cold leftover roasts, cooked vegetables and salads and is added to individual bowls of *bourride*, a Provençal fish soup. Aïoli is also a popular dip for crudités.

all' ALFREDO (IT)
A sauce for pasta, devised and still prepared before the diner's eyes at the Roman restaurant Alfredo alla Scrofa. This style of serving fettuccini has become even more popular abroad. The flat noodles are tossed with an abundance of butter and freshly grated Parmesan cheese. Some versions of the dish now include cream as well as butter.

à l'ALSACIENNE (FR)
In the style of the northeastern province of

Alsace. Whatever dish it applies to is likely to include one or more of the region's three culinary hallmarks: Strasbourg sausage (the familiar fat Knackwurst), ham or sauerkraut.

AMARETTI (IT)

Crisp, tiny biscuits whose name means "little bitters." Amaretti are made from a mixture of the ground kernels of apricot pits (similar to bitter almonds), sugar and egg whites. In most Italian restaurants, they come at the end of a meal, their mildly bittersweet flavor the perfect foil to espresso coffee.

all' AMATRICIANA (IT)

A pasta sauce from the town of Amatrice, near Rome. It is made from tomatoes, olive oil, chopped onion and bacon or salt pork. In Amatrice, the sauce is served over a pasta called bucatini, a thick, long spaghetti with a hole in the middle. Elsewhere, ordinary spaghetti is an appropriate vehicle. Pecorino, a sheep cheese produced in the region, is grated over the sauce at table. If you see a dish called *alla Matriciana*, it is the same.

à l'AMÉRICAINE *or* **à l'AMORICAINE** (FR)

"American style" describes one of the richest of *haute cuisine* lobster dishes. Fresh lobster is cut up and sautéed in olive oil, then simmered with tomatoes, white wine, garlic, onions, shallots and herbs. The liquid is then drained off and turned into a sauce with the lobster's coral (ROE) and liver, butter, cayenne and dashes of brandy and lemon juice. The same sauce served over eggs or other fish is also called à l'Américaine.

AMORINI

See PASTAS.

ANGELS ON HORSEBACK (UK)

A whimsical name for fresh oysters wrapped in bacon and broiled or grilled. They may be served as an appetizer with drinks or as a first course, but in a traditional British meal they would more likely be served as a "savoury"—a light, nonsweet course following the dessert.

11

à l'ANGLAISE (FR)

"English style" applies to very simply cooked dishes of mutton, poultry, fish or vegetables: They may be poached in water, *court bouillon* or stock. Fish with this label are also sometimes grilled with butter or oil, and potatoes may be peeled and steamed. *Crème anglaise* is French for "custard."

ANOLINI

See PASTA.

ANTICUCHOS (LA)

A specialty of Peru, these are skewered cubes of beef heart that have been marinated overnight in vinegar, then grilled and basted with hot chili sauce. Eaten as a snack or appetizer, they're found everywhere, from cocktail parties to street-corner stands.

ARABIC COOKING

See MIDDLE EASTERN COOKING.

ARGENTEUIL (FR)

The name of a region near Paris that grows remarkably good white asparagus. Any sauté of meat, poultry or seafood garnished with that delicacy, or even with green asparagus, may well bear the region's name; so may cream of asparagus soup.

à l'ARLÉSIENNE (FR)

Arles is a city in Provence, the Mediterranean region where sun-ripened tomatoes are abundant. Arles-style garnishes for meat, poultry or seafood always include tomatoes. In one version, tomatoes are stuffed with rice and accompanied by olives, anchovies and potatoes; another sautées them with onions and eggplant; a third garnish uses tomatoes stewed with hearts of endive.

ARRABIATA (IT)

"Raging" with hot red peppers. This tomato sauce is usually served with the variety of PASTA called penne.

ASPIC

The word may well derive from "asp," a chilling, shivery serpent. When a clear, gelatin-rich stock of meat, poultry or fish is chilled, it sets into shimmering aspic. Spooned over cold foods while still liquid, the aspic makes an attractive glaze. Whole hard-boiled eggs or cooked mixed vegetables are often molded in aspic as hors d'oeuvres or salads. Decoratively cut or roughly chopped pieces of aspic garnish formal cold platters—perhaps a whole poached salmon or a PÂTÉ. Aspic is sometimes flavored with wine, sherry or port or blended with tomato purée; mixed with cream and egg yolks, it becomes a CHAUD FROID sauce.

AURORA sauce (FR)

A red-hued sauce; named for the goddess of the dawn—a mixture of tomato purée and VELOUTÉ, served on hardboiled eggs and on poached chicken or sweetbreads.

AUSTRIAN COOKING

See GERMAN COOKING.

AVGOLEMONO (GR)

Avgo in Greek means "egg"; *lemono,* "lemon." This thick sauce is made by whisking together eggs and lemon juice, then adding a little broth. Fish, meat or poultry broth may be used, depending on the main course the rich, tart sauce will grace. You may get avgolemono sauce served with Greek stuffed cabbage rolls, with roast chicken or with meatballs.

Avgolemono soup is any broth—but usually chicken—to which the sauce is added.

B

The pleasures of the table belong to all ages, to all conditions, to all countries and to every day. They can be associated with all the other pleasures and remain the longest to console us for the loss of the rest.
—JEAN ANTHELME BRILLAT-SAVARIN

BABA (EE)

King Stanislas I of Poland reputedly invented this spongy, yeast-raised, sometimes currant-studded cake, baked in a turban-shaped mold. Inspired by its shape, he named it for his favorite character in fiction, Ali Baba of *A Thousand and One Nights.* The baba is most often soaked with a rum syrup before serving, becoming a *baba au rhum;* its heady sweetness is best when cut with a cup of espresso or cappuccino.

BABA GHANOOSH (ME)

This cold hors d'oeuvre purée of eggplant with garlic, lemon, TAHINI (sesame-seed paste) and olive oil has a voluptuous texture that goes some way toward explaining its name (which means "harem girl"); in tune with its image, it may be adorned with baublelike garnishes of pomegranate seeds and chopped mint. Before the eggplant is puréed, it is roasted over an open flame, which gives the spread a smoky flavor.

BACALAO or BACALHAU (IB)

The name for dried salt-cod found throughout the Iberian peninsula. Reconstituted and de-salted by a half-day's soak in water or milk, it can be prepared in a variety of ways: simmered simply with olive oil and garlic or with more substantial accompaniments like tomatoes, peppers, onions and salt pork; or mashed with potatoes, breadcrumbs and eggs, then fried as codfish cakes. The popularity of salt-cod dishes in Catholic Iberia and Latin America is easily explained: in times past, it was the only sure source of Friday fish for inland dwellers.

BAGNA CAUDA (IT)

A "hot bath" is how the natives of the Piedmont region describe this thick, hot dip of chopped anchovies, garlic, olive oil, butter and white TRUFFLE, served with raw vegetables and crusty bread or breadsticks. The pungent dip keeps warm at the table over an alcohol burner or other convenient heat source. If you sample a bagna cauda in its native region, you will dip in it the local cardoon, or thistle.

BAKLAVA (ME/GR)

Byzantine in origin, this is an extravagant, layered concoction of PHYLLO pastry, chopped nuts, butter and spices, drenched after baking with a honey syrup that may be scented with rose water. Prepared in a large sheet pan, the finished baklava is cut into diamond-shaped individual servings. The pastry's rich,

15

sweet flavor is nicely complemented by a strong, thick Greek- or Turkish-style coffee.

BALLOTTINE (FR)

Means "little bundle." It's the name for boned poultry—and less often meat or fish—spread with a fine, herbed-sausage stuffing (or, in the case of fish, with a MOUSSELINE), rolled up and compactly tied, then poached or braised. The roll is served hot, in slices, with a selection of vegetable garnishes and a sauce made from the cooking liquid. It is often confused with the classic cold preparation known as a GALANTINE.

BARQUETTES (FR)

The word means "little boats," referring to oval shells of crisp puff or shortcrust pastry that can do duty in every course of a meal.

à la BASQUAISE (FR)

"In the Basque style" describes a garnish for meat or poultry that features Bayonne ham—a Basque specialty—along with *cèpes* (see MUSHROOMS) and diced potato.

BASTOURMA

See PASTOURMA.

BAVAROIS (FR)

Known in English as "Bavarian cream," it is a classic dessert named by a long-forgotten French chef on a Bavarian estate. Its voluptuous mixture of custard, gelatin and whipped cream is packed into a round, sculptural mold, chilled in the refrigerator until set and then unmolded. The mixture may be flavored and colored in many different ways, with chocolate, coffee, fruit purées, liqueurs, candied fruits or nuts; differently colored and flavored mixtures are often combined in the same mold for an especially beautiful presentation. Well known as the Bavarois is as a custard-based dessert, it is intriguing to note that in its earliest versions, the mixture was bound not with egg yolks but with isinglass, a gelatin made from the air bladders of fish.

BAVETTE

See PASTA.

BAYONNE HAM
See HAMS.

BÉARNAISE (FR)
A suave amalgam of egg yolks, butter, white wine, vinegar, shallots and tarragon composes this classic sauce for steaks and other grilled meats. Despite its name, it did not originate in the southwestern province of Béarn. It was invented in the early nineteenth century at the Pavillon Henry IV, a restaurant near Paris, and was named to honor King Henry IV, a native of Béarn.

BÉCHAMEL (FR)
Invented by Louis de Béchameil, a seventeenth-century financier who served as Louis XIV's royal steward, it is a classic sauce in its own right and the basis for many other rich, creamy sauces. The basic béchamel sauce is made by mixing a *roux* (equal amounts of butter and flour cooked together) with heated milk, simmering the sauce until it thickens. With Gruyère, Parmesan and cream added, it becomes a MORNAY sauce; a PIEMONTAISE sauce, used over chicken, blends béchamel with butter-stewed onions, diced white TRUFFLES and pine nuts. A thick béchamel may also bind the filling for chicken or seafood crêpes. Poured over pieces of meat or vegetables that are then briefly baked or broiled, the béchamel becomes the brown crust of a GRATIN.

BEGGAR'S CHICKEN (CH)
This classic dish of China's coastal regions involves smearing a chicken with a thick coating of clay. Baked until the clay sets to a hard crust, the chicken is brought to the table, as if petrified. The clay is broken with a hammer or mallet, revealing a most succulent chicken inside—all its juices having been sealed in.

BELUGA CAVIAR
See ROES.

BENEDICT (US)
The sauce that makes eggs benedict. On top of a toasted English muffin goes sliced

smoked ham or Canadian bacon; on top of that, a poached egg. The finishing touch is a hot HOLLANDAISE sauce.

BERLINERWURST

See WURSTS.

BEURRE BLANC (FR)

So-called white butter is a classic sauce for poached fish. Shallots are simmered in wine vinegar until the mixture reduces to a tart essence; then cubes of butter are whisked in, and the warm, creamy sauce is poured over the fish.

BEURRE NOIR (FR)

A brown butter sauce made by heating the butter until it foams up and colors, then adding parsley, capers and a hint of vinegar. The name means ''black butter.'' The sauce is best with such simple poached or pan-fried foods as eggs, vegetables or fish. It is most elegant with brains or sweetbreads.

BHELPURI (IN)

An immensely popular snack, sold by street vendors throughout India—and even at stands set up on the beaches of Bombay. Crisp puffed rice is tossed together with whole toasted lentils, peanuts, chopped onion, coriander leaves, sweet CHUTNEY and noodles made with chick-pea flour to make an appetite-satisfying dish, combining crunchy textures with sweet, sour and salty tastes.

BIERWURST

See WURSTS.

BIGARADE SAUCE (FR)

It usually dresses roast duck, combining the roasting juices with a little caramelized sugar and the juice of bitter Seville oranges, or bigarades. With more tart character than a sauce made from ordinary oranges, it makes a dish that is a far cry from the usual, syrupy-sweet *canard à l'orange* served at many mediocre French restaurants.

BIGOS (EE)

This ''hunter's stew'' is the national dish of Poland. It originated as the ideal meal for hunting parties, its stewing pot a receptacle for any available game and vegetables. Today, it has evolved into a slightly more formal combination of fresh pork, beef, game, hams and sausages—particularly KIELBASA—simmered with sauerkraut, apples, onions and tomatoes in Madeira and stock. In effect, it is the Eastern European cousin to the grand French CHOUCROUTE. Fresh cabbage is sometimes substituted for the sauerkraut.

BIRD'S NEST SOUP (CH)

Not one of those dishes named with poetic whimsy, it really is made from the nests of swiftlets, delicate dried structures that the birds construct with a substance they make by dissolving seaweed with their saliva. The nests, simmered in chicken broth with minced chicken, dissolve to a sublime, lightly gelatinous concoction.

BIRIANI (IN)

Introduced to India by the Moguls in the sixteenth century, this one-dish meal combines cooked saffron-scented rice with a mildly spiced dry braise of meat, poultry, seafood, eggs or vegetables. Birianis may be as simple or special as the restaurants they are ordered in: a first-class one will serve them gloriously decked with fried onions, egg slices, currants, tomato wedges and even tissue-thin edible silver foil, a favorite decoration in more expensive Indian restaurants. A light curried gravy or mixed vegetable curry is served alongside to moisten the rice. The best birianis are made using *basmati* rice, a long-grain rice that has a special aroma of nuts and milk.

BISCUIT TORTONI (IT)

Tortoni was the family name of an eighteenth-century Neapolitan father-and-son team of confectioners and ice-cream makers. Besides their marvelous varieties of GRANITA, they are remembered for the son's biscuit tortoni, a featured dessert in many Italian cafés to this day. It is an exquisite frozen concoction of whipped cream, beaten egg whites, sugar and powdered roasted almonds—more a mousse than an ice cream.

BISMARCK

See HERRINGS.

BISQUE (FR)

Most commonly, any kind of puréed soup based on shellfish—particularly crayfish, lobster or crab. The true bisque has a smooth texture and is lightly thickened with cream or egg yolks, though not always. Beware of the gummy imitations made using cream thickened with flour. Cream of tomato soup is sometimes erroneously called bisque only because the word has also come to mean pink in color. During the eighteenth century, a bisque might also have been made using pigeon or quail meat and thickened with breadcrumbs. To be sick and forbidden to eat bisque, a French wit punned, *je bisque en y songeant* ("I am vexed even to dream of it").

BLACK BUN (UK)

So called because it has so much candied fruits, nuts and ground spices kneaded into its egg-and-butter yeast dough that it is almost black in color inside. The fruitcake dough, shaped in a large, flat round, is always wrapped in a thin layer of plain dough before baking, so it looks like a plain loaf until it is sliced. The bun, cut in wedges, is spread with butter and served with tea.

BLACK PUDDING (UK)

Also known as "blood sausage" and popular in France as *boudin noir,* it is a centuries-old dish prepared traditionally at the start of winter when the fattened pigs are slaughtered to provide meat for the coming cold months. A British recipe from 1600 in the *English Housewife's Book* accurately describes one version: "small otemeale mixed with blood, and the liver of either sheep, calf or swine." Today the normal ingredients are pig's blood, oatmeal, finely minced pork fat, onions and herbs. In the north of England, they use generous amounts of pennyroyal, a relative of mint. The sausages are precooked by boiling, but they are usually served sliced and pan-fried. Similar sausages can be found throughout Europe.

BLAFF (CARIB)

A favorite seafood dish of the islands, it consists of a firm-fleshed white fish poached quickly in a fragrant, spicy wine-and-water broth—with allspice, cloves, garlic, scallions, peppercorns, hot red chilies and lots of fresh lime.

BLANCMANGE (FR)

The name means "something white to eat," but this is hardly an adequate description for this sublime molded dessert of sweetened milk infused with the essence of pulverized almonds, gelatin and whipped cream. The great nineteenth-century chef and author Carême declared that the gentle almond flavor in blancmange made it "just right for sweetening the bitterness of humors."

BLANQUETTE (FR)

The term is a diminutive of *blanc*, "white." It refers basically to a country braise of light meat—veal, young lamb or chicken—with baby onions, mushrooms and a sauce of VE-LOUTÉ bound with egg yolks and cream. It is a rich, thick concoction, best served over boiled white rice.

au BLEU (FR)

A method of cooking freshwater fish, especially trout. The fish's skin has a delicate natural coating that turns a translucent blue when it is poached in water to which vinegar has been added. Only freshly killed trout can be cooked *au bleu*; the crucial coating deteriorates within hours after the fish leaves the water. In the finest restaurants, the fish is kept alive until the moment it is cooked.

BLINI (RUS)

Similar to crêpes,these small, thin Russian pancakes are made from a yeast-leavened buckwheat-flour batter. Spread with butter or sour cream, they are the classic vehicle for caviar; but they are just as appropriate wrapped around or topped with other roes, smoked fish, pickled herring, chopped mushrooms and onions, or homemade preserves. During the traditional Russian pre-Lenten feasts, whole meals may be built around blini, each diner consuming a dozen or more with a variety of accompaniments.

BLINTZ (JE)

The word has its root in the Russian BLINI. These egg-batter crêpes are folded around a filling and sautéed in butter until golden. They make a perfect simple main dish at any time. Classic blintzes contain sweetened farmer cheese or pot cheese and are served with sour cream or preserves; but like any crêpe assembly, modern versions may instead contain potatoes, fish, meat, poultry or stewed fruits. Today, to get the traditional version, it is necessary to order "cheese blintzes," a phrase that, according to the Jewish-American writer Leo Rosten, "once would have sounded as redundant as 'wet water.' "

BLOATER

See HERRINGS.

BLOOD SAUSAGE

See BLACK PUDDING.

BLUTWURST

See WURSTS.

BOBOTIE (AF)

A homey casserole that displays an amalgam of influences—Dutch, Asian and English.

Ground beef or lamb is cooked with curry spices, lemon, a touch of sugar, raisins and almonds. Transferred to a casserole, the meat is topped with a mixture of beaten egg and milk, then baked until its custardlike surface sets, turning a light golden brown.

BOCKWURST

See WURSTS.

BOLETUS

See MUSHROOMS.

BOLLITO MISTO (IT)

This ''mixed boil'' is a typically hearty main course—not unlike a boiled-beef dinner—from the Piedmont region abutting the Alpines of France and Switzerland. Tongue, chuck roast, veal, chicken and ham are simmered together with carrots, onions, celery, herbs and spices. The cooking broth may be served as a first course, garnished with tiny pasta. Then the cooked meats are carved and served, joined by a garlic sausage that has been poached separately to keep its fat out of the broth. Served on the side to spice up the meats is a pungent cold green sauce (*salsa verde*) of capers, garlic, shallots, anchovies, olive oil and lemon juice.

BOLOGNESE sauce (IT)

The preeminent spaghetti topping from Bologna, also called RAGÙ. It is a hearty mixture of one or several chopped meats—beef, pork, chicken liver, prosciutto (see HAMS)—with tomatoes, onions, garlic, mushrooms, wine and herbs. A true Bolognese sauce should be chunky with meat, unlike the thin, meat-speckled glop passed off by some Italian restaurants in the United States.

BOMBE (FR)

A classic frozen ice-cream dessert, it is so named because of the projectile-shaped mold in which it is frozen. All bombes contain at least two kinds of ice cream or sorbet, differing in flavor and texture and forming concentric layers in the mold. Some possibilities are creamy vanilla or chocolate ice cream;

slightly grainy ices of puréed raspberries, apricots or citrus fruits; and light frozen mousses of coffee, chocolate or fruit. Once the bombe has set solid in the freezer, it is unmolded onto a chilled platter and cut into wedges for serving.

BONNE FEMME (FR)

Literally "good woman," the term describes a simple home-style garnish as mother might make it: potatoes, onions, mushrooms and bacon for a sautéed chicken; just mushroom slices for a pan-fried or poached piece of fish.

à la BORDELAISE (FR)

"Bordeaux style." It refers to a grilled meat dish finished with a sauce made from the wine of that region, along with DEMI-GLACE, herbs and shallots. Cubes of poached beef marrow are the classic garnish.

BÖREK (ME)

A popular Turkish dish, it is made with PHYLLO pastry, wrapped around garlic-flavored goat cheese, spicy chopped beef or lamb or chopped vegetables. As an hors d'oeuvre, they are usually served as thin, cigarlike tubes, appropriately called *cigara bořek*. Larger, rectangular packages may be served as a main course. Occasionally, the dough is also filled with chopped nuts or sweetened cheese to make dessert pastries.

BORNHOLM HERRING

See HERRINGS.

BOTVINYA (RUS)

An elegant, chilled soup of shredded sorrel (a tart-flavored relative of spinach) or spinach, with pieces of freshly poached sturgeon or salmon, in a broth liberally spiked with a sour grain liquor called *kvass*. Extra sparkle comes from a splash of Champagne or a dash of sherry at serving time; sour cream may be added to individual portions if more smoothness is desired.

BOUILLABAISE (FR)

The fishermen of the Mediterranean port of Marseilles invented this generous lunchtime stew or soup that includes whatever seafood is in the day's catch. Upwards of a dozen different kinds of sea creatures may find their way into a bouillabaise: firm white fish such as halibut, snapper, haddock and cod; meaty, oily chunks of eel; mussels, scallops or clams; and even lobster, though some traditionalists might exclude it. All Marseillais agree, though, that the stew is nothing without *rascasse* (John Dory, in English); this ugly, spiny fish has mild white flesh that has little character on its own but that, through some culinary alchemy, enhances a bouillabaise's flavor. (The porgy is the best substitute available in America.) The fish is simmered in a white wine *court bouillon* laden with the tomatoes, garlic and olive oil abundant in Provence, as well as saffron, onions, leeks, fennel and dried orange peel.

à la BOUQUETIÈRE (FR)

In a flower-girl's style charmingly describes a classic garnish for roast meat. A bouquet of garden produce, it consists of buttered peas and green beans, cauliflower florets with HOLLANDAISE, small ovals of sautéed potatoes, and artichoke bottoms filled with diced carrot and turnip, all artfully displayed around the whole or sliced joint of meat.

à la BOURGEOISE (FR)

Despite the word's modern negative connotation, the truest translation in culinary terms is "home-style." A large cut of beef, or some other meat or poultry, is stewed with two of the vegetables most commonly found in the family larder—carrots and onions (and sometimes celery and turnips, too). Diced lean bacon adds to its savor.

à la BOURGUIGNONNE (FR)

"In the style of Burgundy." It is a sauce that makes use of that region's full-bodied red wines as a braising liquid—particularly for beef. *Boeuf à la bourguignonne* is garnished with mushrooms, baby onions and cubes of bacon or pork belly; without bacon, the same garnishes accompany fish cooked in Burgundy's wine.

BRADENHAM HAM
See HAMS.

BRATWURST
See WURSTS.

BRAUNSCHWEIGER
See WURSTS.

à la BRETONNE (FR)

The phrase describes two different preparations from Brittany. One involves the white beans (*haricots blancs*) common in the region. Bathed in an oniony meat-stock sauce, they are used to garnish roasted or braised meats served in this style; puréed and thinned with stock into a soup, they become a *purée Bretonne*. Fish cooked à la Bretonne, however, has a beanless sauce of white wine, butter, carrots, onions, celery and leeks; with cream instead of wine, this *sauce Bretonne* may also dress light meats.

BRIOCHE (FR)

A bread that comes as close to being cake as bread can come, packed as its dough is with eggs and butter. Baked in large or individual-size fluted molds, brioches are usually graced with small topknots that give them the name *brioches à têtes*—brioches with heads. They are wonderful at breakfast, with butter, jam and *café au lait*. Large or small brioches are also hollowed out and used as edible containers for savory stews of meat, poultry or fish. Large, fresh country sausage is sometimes wrapped in a thin casing of the dough, then baked and sliced, becoming the luncheon dish *saucisson en brioche*.

BRITISH COOKING

Overdone roasts and soggy vegetables: that's how the food of the British Isles is often characterized. It is an image many modern British restaurants do little to shake, but it's far from the truth. Several centuries ago, the French actually looked to British cooking with admiration, and examples of the cooking they admired can still be found by the diligent diner. It is possible to find perfectly cooked examples of the classic rib roast of beef with YORKSHIRE PUDDING, the leg of lamb with mint sauce or the loin of pork with apple sauce. They suggest a country heartiness and homeyness that extends throughout the nation's most traditional foods. Steak and kidney pie is an excellent example: at its best, it combines a thick stew of cubed beefsteak, finely minced veal kidney and—in the most elegant versions—freshly shucked oysters in a shortcrust or flaky pastry casing. On a more everyday level, there are country-style dishes such as the combination of sausage and Yorkshire pudding called TOAD-IN-THE-HOLE; the various JUGGED game stews; or the lunchtime specialty from Cornwall, the Cornish PASTY. From Wales, there is the classic hot cheese dish, Welsh rabbit. Scotland contributes such delights as the main-course soup called COCK-A-LEEKIE; SCOTCH EGGS, a popular pub food; and the sausage immortalized by the poet Robert Burns, haggis. English country sausages are excellent: one, BLACK PUDDING, outclasses similar varieties produced in France and Germany. Other notable British dishes show the influence of the nation's colonial past in India: MULLIGATAWNY SOUP and KEDGEREE have Indian-derived names, and along with Worcestershire sauce they exhibit subtle spicing from the subcontinent. British desserts display the same emphasis on country goodness. Most famous of these is the abundant assembly of cream, cake, custard, fruit and sherry, humbly known as TRIFLE. Another unassumingly named dessert, luscious yet homey and simple, is the cream-and-fruit purée called FOOL. In traditional British meals, desserts are followed by a ''savoury'' course such as a Welsh rabbit or ANGELS ON HORSEBACK. The British also make fine dining out of meals to which other nations give short shrift. Teatime calls for fine baked goods like Sally Lunn, SCONES, CRUMPETS and BLACK BUN, with homemade preserves and CLOTTED CREAM. Breakfast can become a generous feast, with eggs accompanied by bacon, sausages, crumpets, scones and more substantial dishes such as kedgeree or some of the country's renowned smoked fish, such as KIPPERS or FINNAN HADDIE. The gourmet who discounts or ignores British cooking will miss such unique pleasures.

BUBBLE AND SQUEAK (UK)

This hash of beef, potato and cabbage or brussels sprouts, pan fried until brown and crusty, is traditionally made on Monday from Sunday dinner leftovers; sometimes vegetables alone are used, the only trace of meat being the suet used for frying. The name comes from the sound the mixture makes as it cooks.

BUCATINI

See PASTA.

BUDDHA'S DELIGHT

See MONK'S VEGETABLES.

BUÑUELOS (MEX)

Lighter and less rich than CHURROS, these puffed pastries are rolled out flat, cut into squares or circles and fried in hot lard until puffy. Once drained, they are dusted with cinnamon sugar. Like *churros*, they are eaten for breakfast or as a snack, with coffee or hot chocolate.

C

When there is no more cookery in the world there will be no more letters, no quick and lofty intelligence, no pleasant easy relationships, no more social unity.
—MARIE-ANTOINE CARÊME

alla CACCIATORE (IT)

"Hunter's style" usually describes meat, poultry or seafood cooked in tomato and wine sauce. A treatment popular in the south, it is often elaborated with scallions, mushrooms, peppers, garlic and herbs. Less often, the same word is used for a sauce based on anchovies, garlic and olive oil, usually served with lamb.

CALALOO (CARIB)

The most cherished soup of the Antilles, it is based on a vegetable known by the same name, a relative of such inedible plants as philodendrons and calla lilies. The plant was carried to the Caribbean from Africa, and the soup reflects that origin with its other main vegetable, okra. The ingredients include sharp-flavored calaloo leaves, garlic, onions, cloves, herbs, chili peppers, a cooking liquid of chicken broth and coconut milk, and such optional extras as salt pork, bananas, salt cod and crabmeat. The ingredients are simmered

together and, in the native style, beaten by
hand with a wooden stick called a *baton lélé*.

jambon de CAMPAGNE

See HAMS.

pâté de CAMPAGNE

See PÂTÉ.

CANNELONI

See PASTA.

CANNOLI (IT)

A Sicilian treat, consisting of a tube of fried or
baked wine-flavored pastry, filled with a ricotta cream, chocolate chips and candied
fruit. Saracen invaders brought the pastries'
ancestors to Sicily in the ninth century. Because the natives often called the invaders
"Turks," these pastries were first named
cappelli di turco, or Turk's hats.

CANNOLICCHI

See PASTA.

CANTONESE COOKING

See CHINESE COOKING.

CAPONATA *or* **CAPONATINA** (IT)

Sicily's answer to RATATOUILLE. "He who has
not eaten a caponatina of eggplant," noted
one Sicilian gourmet, "has never reached the
antechamber of the terrestrial paradise."
This sweet-sour vegetable stew, served either hot or cold as an antipasto, features
eggplant, celery, black olives and capers in a
sauce of tomatoes, vinegar and sugar. Cooks
in Palermo add pine nuts to the mixture.
Others may add anything from octopus to
chocolate.

CAPPELLETTI

See PASTA.

alla CARBONARA (IT)

Charcoal-makers, so the name tells us, are
responsible for this style of tossing pasta with
bacon or salt pork, olive oil, raw eggs, Parmesan cheese and freshly ground black pepper. The heat of the pasta cooks the egg,
gently binding the mixture.

CARBONNADE (BNL)

A stew of beef, caramelized onions and dark

beer. Its full name is *carbonnade à la fla-mande,* and it is served with boiled potatoes or noodles. To harmonize with the sauce, a glass of beer is the appropriate drink.

CARIBBEAN COOKING

African, British, French, Spanish, Portuguese, Indian, Dutch: So many different peoples have settled in these islands that the cuisine, naturally featuring seafoods and tropical fruits and vegetables, is a carnival of tastes, textures and colors. The influences of all the outside cuisines can be found—there is Indian curry, Portuguese BACA-LAO, French POT-AU-FEU, English PASTY-like turnovers. But here the curry might include taro root, papaya and pumpkin or a dash of rum; the bacalao might be used to stuff breadfruit or be tossed in a salad with hot chilies, tomatoes, onion and avocado; the pot-au-feu will include bananas and sweet potatoes; the pasties, renamed "patties," will have a hot, peppery meat filling. Exciting though such variations are, it is worth seeking out Caribbean originals as well: the hearty fish stew called BLAFF, for example, or the spicy, creamy soup with the lullabylike name of CALALOO.

CARPACCIO (IT)

Very thin slices of raw tenderloin. Invented at Harry's Bar in Venice, this hors d'oeuvre or light main course is made of raw prime beef sliced or pounded to translucent thinness, which may explain why it was named after the fifteenth-century Venetian painter whose canvasses captured the crystalline light of that city's sea and sky. In any case, the beef is garnished with piquant condiments such as capers, salted anchovies, pimientos, chopped chives, scallions and Dijon mustard.

CARPETBAG STEAK (AUS)

A thick, top-quality steak is slit open horizontally to form a pocket, then stuffed with freshly shelled raw oysters—packed as full as a carpetbag. Grilled over charcoal, the steak may be served as one whole serving or cut into thick slices for several diners.

CASSATA (IT)

The name applies to two different festive desserts. If the word appears alone, it means a molded ice cream, similar to the French BOMBE: the mold is lined with chocolate or a very dense, hard ice cream; softer, contrasting flavors and colors of ice cream are packed inside. If cassata is given the added label *alla Siciliana*, or Sicilian style, no ice cream is involved at all. This is the island's favorite cake. It consists of layers of pound cake separated by a ricotta-cheese filling doctored with liqueur and bits of chocolate and candied fruit, the whole cake coated with dark chocolate frosting and chilled for a day. This rich dessert appears at the most special occasions: weddings, Christmas and Easter.

CASSOULET (FR)

A hearty, voluptuous stew of dried white beans (*haricots blancs*) and fresh and preserved meats. Cassoulet is a centuries-old speciality of the Languedoc region of southern France, where three towns claim it for their own. Each has its own recipe for the classic dish; but cassoulet is an unabashedly generous dish, and a grand one might well include the preserved goose Toulouse demands, Carcassone's lamb and Castelnaudry's pork, as well as some sausage, mutton or duck. Layered in a casserole, the stew may bake for up to five hours at low heat; the crust that develops on top, repeatedly folded in and allowed to reform, is a requisite of the authentic cassoulet.

CAVIAR

See ROES.

CÈPES

See MUSHROOMS.

CERVELAS (FR)

A relatively mild variety of sausage, made from pork and pork fat, sometimes lightly flavored with garlic and pepper. The sausage is air-cured for a day or two, to give it a firm texture, but it still must be cooked—poached in water—before it is eaten. The name is applied fairly freely to any sausage that meets these general requirements, but there is room for variation: one type of cervelas popular in Lyons, for example, includes whole pistachio nuts and pieces of black TRUFFLE. In fact, the sausage as it is known today evolved from the original cervelas, probably once made from brains.

CERVELAT (GE)

Related to the French CERVELAS mainly in name. It is a heftier sausage than its cousin from the southwest, including beef with the pork. Smoke-cured, it requires no cooking. It is usually eaten sliced, as a cold cut.

CEVICHE *or* **CEBICHE** (LA)

One of the world's great pickled dishes, it consists of fish ''cooked'' without the benefit of heat. Small cubes of firm-fleshed white fish fillets—*corvina* (similar to striped bass), sole, sea scallops, conch and shrimp are good choices—are mixed with chilies, onions, garlic and seasonings and covered with lime and lemon juice. Over the course of several hours, the citric acid in the juices virtually cooks the delicate pieces of fish: they turn firm, opaque and white. The fish is served cold on a bed of lettuce, often garnished with cold niblets of corn and chunks of sweet potato. Peruvian in origin, ceviche is often claimed as the national dish of several other Latin American countries, and each has its

33

own variations—in Ecuador, for example, they replace lemon and lime juice with the juice of bitter Seville oranges.

CHALUPA (MEX)

The word means "canoe," referring to the shape of these oval TORTILLAS with raised rims. Fried until crisp, they are filled with chicken or pork, cheese and chili sauce. Do not confuse them with *chalupines,* or fried crickets, a popular food in the southern state of Oaxaca.

CHAMP (IR)

A homey preparation of mashed potatoes with scallions and milk. What makes it special is the well filled with melted butter at each serving's center; forkful by forkful, the champ is dipped into the butter and eaten.

CHANTERELLES

See MUSHROOMS.

CHAPATI (IN)

India's everyday bread, an unleavened whole-wheat dough rolled into very thin pancakes and cooked without fat on a hot griddle, much like the Mexican TORTILLA. The plain bread rounds make a nice contrast to rich curries that contain a lot of butter or cream, but they are most often eaten as part of simpler, lighter meals.

CHARLOTTE (FR)

The name of two different but related desserts, both molded in a round, deep, straight-sided mold called a charlotte. Furit charlottes are made by lining the mold with buttered bread, then filling it with fruit purée—apple charlotte is the traditional choice—and baking it. Other charlottes are cold preparations with cream fillings (as in *charlotte à la* CHANTILLY). Most famous of these is the *charlotte russe,* a treat created in 1815 by the great chef Carême for Czar Alexander I of Russia. In this version, the mold is lined with sponge-cake fingers, filled with BAVARIAN CREAM and chilled until firm. All charlottes are turned out of the mold and cut into wedges for serving.

à la CHASSEUR (FR)

The French "huntsman's style" refers to a white-wine sauce with that most typical and enticing woodland ingredient, mushrooms, mixed with shallots and a little tomato. The sauce is served most often with beef or chicken. Italian huntsmen prefer a different style, *alla* CACCIATORE.

CHAUD-FROID (FR)

"Hot-cold" is the name of this white sauce for cold chicken or game birds. A VELOUTÉ is enriched with cream, and then warmed ASPIC is added to help it set. The finished sauce is used to glaze cold meat, which is then decorated with truffle slices and chopped aspic. Any dish prepared with this sauce is itself known as a chaud-froid. According to culinary legend, the dish was invented in 1759 when the maréchal of Luxembourg was called away from a banquet he was giving by a messenger summoning him to the king's council. When the maréchal finally returned home, he ate some of a FRICASSÉE, long since turned cold; he liked the dish so much that he rechristened it "chaud-froid."

CHAWAN-MUSHI (JA)

An egg soup cooked in individual bowls in a steamer, it becomes a light custard when it sets. Each bowl contains a selection of such delicate ingredients as chicken breast, shrimp, *Shiitake* MUSHROOMS, spinach and scallions; these are topped with a mixture of DASHI and eggs—the custard mixture—and a garnish of thin-sliced lime or lemon. The cooked soup is eaten with a spoon, and the bits of food are plucked out with chopsticks.

CHESS PIE (US)

A variety of pecan pie that includes beaten egg in its filling for a lighter consistency. It is a Southern dessert dating from Civil War times, but in no way does it resemble a chessboard. The name, so a plausible explanation goes, comes from a humble cook's description of the sweet: "It's jus' pie."

CHILAQUILES (MEX)

Stale TORTILLAS are the foundation of this satisfying casserole, making it a favorite with housewives, students and efficiently run restaurants. The tortillas are cut into narrow strips, lightly fried in lard or oil, layered with chili sauce and—in more substantial versions—chopped leftover meat; then the casserole is baked until hot. A salad completes the simple meal.

CHINESE COOKING

What FRENCH COOKING in all its variety is to the West, Chinese is to the East: not one cuisine but several distinct and highly developed styles.

Northern Cuisines. The hub of northern cooking is China's capital, Peking, once the locus of the so-called Mandarin dishes of the imperial court. These include such refined delicacies as SHARK'S FIN SOUP and BIRD'S NEST SOUP and the most famous main course in all Chinese cooking, PEKING DUCK. Both Peking duck and another northern favorite, MOO SHU PORK, are eaten in thin wheat-flour pancakes. In fact, wheat, in the form of pancakes, buns or noodles, is the staple of northern cooking. Other northern provinces include Mongolia, famous for its barbecued lamb and its distinctive version of FIRE POT. Subtle sweet-and-sour dishes are found in the northern provinces of Honan and Shantung, including whole fried carp in sweet-and-sour sauce.

Coastal Cuisines. Soy sauce, rice-wine vinegar and sugar season many of the dishes of Shanghai; soy sauce and paste, fermented shrimp-paste and wine-lees paste (*hang chiao*) distinguish the cooking of Fukien province, to its south. The soy in both of these coastal regions imparts a red color to food braised in it—the designation "red-cooked" thus applies to many coastal dishes. Not surprisingly, seafoods of all kinds are featured, the most notable recipes being SQUIRREL FISH and soused shrimp. There are also rustic, hearty meat specialities such as LION'S HEAD and BEGGAR'S CHICKEN. Rice is the staple.

Inland Cuisines. Szechwan and Hunan citizens dote on the red chili pepper; from an early age, children there eat the fiery things like candy. Chilies impart some degree of fire to virtually all inland dishes, and they are joined often by onions, scallions, garlic and ginger. Cooks there also make great use of the delicate cloud ear fungus, also known as tree ear (see MUSHROOMS). All these various seasonings and ingredients combine to flavor such specialities as HOT AND SOUR SOUP, Szechwan duck (a spicy version of PEKING DUCK), dry-fried string beans with spicy minced pork, chicken with walnuts and the various dishes designated KUNG PAO. Rice is popular, as well as cellophane noodles (transparent noodles of mung bean flour).

Southern Cooking. This is synonymous with Cantonese, the best-known Chinese cuisine in the Western world. Canton, so far from the capital at Peking, was an easy place from which nineteenth-century Chinese could flee their country without government intervention, and the Cantonese carried to the West their typical, lightly seasoned dishes: vegetable combinations like MONK'S VEGETABLES, roast duck and barbecued pork (*char siu*), steamed fish with black-bean sauce, and the delightful luncheon tidbits known as DIM SUM. Rice accompanies most such dishes, and in the form of the gruel called CONGEE, it serves as breakfast for many Cantonese.

CHIRASHIZUKI (JA)

A midpoint between the delights of SUSHI and those of SASHIMI, it is a convenient luncheon dish comprised of a lacquered box loosely filled with rice and decoratively covered with an assortment of beautifully cut pieces of raw fish and pickled vegetables.

CHLODNIK (EE)

A variation on *barszcz,* the Polish BORSCH, this cold summer soup always contains chopped cucumbers and beets, as well as scallions and radishes; other fresh vegetables may be included in season. The soup gets a tart, slightly sweet flavor from lemon juice or vinegar, sour cream and fresh dill. The traditional garnish is always chopped egg. Regional variations may extend the soup with diced veal, crayfish or shrimp.

CHOLENT (JE)

The traditional Sabbath dish, a stew of dried beans; meats such as lamb, beef or chicken; broth; and seasonings. Because orthodox Jews are forbidden to cook on the day of rest, they would carry earthenware crocks of cholent to the local bakery before sundown on Friday and leave them to cook slowly in the dying ovens, to be carried back home and eaten on the Sabbath.

CHORIZO (IB/LA)

The preeminent Spanish sausage, popular in Iberia and throughout Latin America, it is a piquant, oak-smoked mixture of chopped pork; garlic; hot paprika; and sweet red pepper; an inch or more in diameter and in lengths varying from a few inches to a foot or more—and, when tied, often tied in a loop. Cold slices of the sausage are a favorite hors d'oeuvre, alone or as part of a TAPAS array. Its uses in cooking are widespread: It may be grilled, or braised with vegetables or beans, and it appears as an ingredient in PAELLA, COCIDO, omelets and other dishes. In Mexico, chorizo may be found chopped, mixed with tomato and onions and used as a filling for TACOS, ENCHILADAS and other TORTILLA-based dishes. When families make their own chorizo in Extremadura, Spain's west-central region, they also partake of a dish consisting of the seasoned sausage filling alone, sautéed in a pot and eaten communally; the dish is called *la prueba*, or the test, of the chorizo.

CHOUCROUTE (FR)

The name means "sauerkraut," humble and familiar, but when it is a *choucroute garnie,* a garnished suaerkraut in the style of Alsace (*à l' Alsacienne*) or Strasbourg (*à la Strasbourgeoise*), it becomes a noble country dinner.

The pickled cabbage shreds are simmered in broth with good peasant meats—sausages, ham, bacon—along with rich goose fat and onions for several hours to mingle the heady flavors. It is served heaped on a platter with boiled potatoes or a purée of yellow peas.

CHOWDER (US)

A chunky seafood soup, it is a descendant of such French fish soups as BOUILLABAISE. Its name pays homage to that descent, being derived from the French *chaudière* (literally, "heater"), the vessel in which such fisherman's soups were cooked. Like the famed French soup-stew, chowder may include a mixed catch of seafoods, but the best-known version is clam chowder, which is found in two distinct types: New England-style has a mild milk- or cream-based broth with cubes of potato and pieces of onion and salt pork; Manhattan style is made with tomatoes, water, onions and carrots, though it may also include potatoes and other vegetables.

CHUTNEY (IN)

Chutneys are served as relishes beside most curries and other Indian dishes. Dozens of different chutneys exist, based on fruits, vegetables or herbs, raw, cooked or preserved.

Some examples: sweet pickled mangoes (*aam chatni*); grated coconut with coriander leaves, green chilies and mustard seeds, moistened with yogurt and *ghee* (*narial chatni*); chopped raw onions, chilies, coriander and tomato (*kachoomar*); and fresh mint mixed with chilies, onion, ginger, sugar and lemon (*podina chatni*). The choice of which chutney to eat with which main dish is a matter of individual taste; no hard rules exist. One joy of an Indian restaurant meal is the chutney tray, a selection of from two to a dozen or so relishes from which to choose.

CIOPPINO (US)

The Italian immigrant fishermen of San Francisco, California, get credit for this relative of the classic Mediterranean fish stew, BOUILLA-BAISE. The name is an italianization of the English "chip in": the cook chips into the stewpot whatever fish he has, along with olive oil, onions, peppers, tomatoes, herbs, red wine and fish stock. The stew is served in soup bowls, with a sourdough bread to sop up the sauce.

CLAFOUTIS (FR)

This rustic pastry from the Limousin region is made by pouring a sweet batter of eggs, flour and milk into a buttered baking dish full of fresh seasonal fruits, then baking it until golden brown. Cherries are traditional, but plums, apples or grapes are also appropriate. The clafoutis is eaten warm, dusted with confectioner's sugar.

CLOTTED CREAM (UK)

Also known as Cornish cream or Devonshire cream, this English treat is made by cooling scalded, unpasteurized cream; the result is spreadably thick and sweet, tasting slightly of boiled milk. Clotted cream is served in place of butter with teatime scones and jam or poured over fresh berries.

CLOUD EAR FUNGUS

See MUSHROOMS.

COCK-A-LEEKIE (UK)

The name sums up the two main ingredients of this Scottish soup: a stewing fowl (now more likely a hen) and leeks are simmered together, sometimes with oatmeal or prunes. Served as a first course, the soup may contain just broth and leeks or the chicken may be sliced and included to make a main course.

COEUR À LA CRÈME (FR)

Literally a "cream heart," this is a provincial fresh cream cheese molded in a heart-shaped container. It is usually eaten as a teatime treat or for dessert, sprinkled with sugar, drizzled with fresh cream and decorated with berries.

COLCANNON (IR)

An elaboration on CHAMP, this dish adds cabbage to the basic mashed potatoes and scallions. It is served traditionally at All Hallow's Eve, when into the mixture are folded miniature charms that are supposed to foretell the future of those who receive them: a silver sixpence for fortune, a wedding ring for a happy marriage, a thimble for spinsterhood, a button for bachelorhood and a horseshoe for good luck.

CONCHIGLIE

See PASTA.

COQ AU VIN (FR)

The authentic version of this provincial stew is made with pieces of a tough, flavorful old farmyard cock. First they are browned, with MIREPOIX, in a little bacon fat or oil, then simmered in good country red wine and veal stock for several hours, until the meat becomes tender and takes on the tawny color of the liquid—which itself reduces to a syrupy sauce. Before serving, the stew is flambéed with Cognac, and sautéed baby onions, small chunks of carrot and cubes of bacon are folded in. Garlic croutons, often cut into elongated heart shapes called *dents de loup* (wolf's teeth), complete the presentation. In most restaurants today, dishes billed as coq au vin are more likely to be *poulet au vin*, chicken; the meat won't have as much flavor, but cooked in the authentic style, it should still have a rich winey savor and color, good sauce and the proper garnishes.

CORDON BLEU[1] (FR)

The phrase, which translates roughly as "blue ribbon," is commonly used today to describe a good cook or skilled French cookery, usages that distort the origin of the phrase. As history explains it, King Louis XV of France firmly believed in the superiority of male cooks and in the discernment of his own palate. Madame du Barry, to fool the king, had a woman chef cook his dinner one evening, without telling him. He enjoyed the meal with gusto and asked to meet the chef. Madame du Barry introduced her triumphantly and, to honor this woman's feat, asked the king to bestow on her the Royal Order of Saint Esprit—the *cordon bleu*. Since that time, the cordon bleu has been the mark of distinguished female chefs. In recent years, a French cooking school has adopted the name; but neither the name of a single school of cooking nor a very specific honor should be equated with skill or creativity in the kitchen.

CORDON BLEU[2] (SW)

May refer to one specific veal dish, a cutlet stuffed with ham and Emmenthal cheese, breaded and then sautéed in butter.

CORNICHONS (FR)

Midget pickled cucumbers, the classic accompaniment to PÂTÉ and country dishes such as POT AU FEU and POULE-AU-POT. They are made from the same kind of cucumbers used for large pickles, but picked when no more than 1½ inches long. The cucumbers are soaked for several months in vinegar with garlic, onion, pepper and coriander. They should be firm and crisp, with a spicy flavor.

COTECHINO (IT)

A large, fresh pork sausage from the Emilia-Romagna, the region of Bologna. It is distinguished by the inclusion of chopped pork rind, which makes the sausage, once boiled, sublimely succulent and gelatinous (and gives the sausage its name, from *cotenna,* meaning "pig skin"). Seasonings are usually very simple—just salt and pepper—though some versions may be scented with garlic or even, surprisingly, vanilla. In rustic fashion, the sausage is eaten with puréed lentils, and it also finds its way into BOLLITO MISTO.

COULIS (FR)

An inexact word, but one often found on menus. Originally, it was synonymous with sauce, any sauce, and with the cooking juices of roast meat. Now, it generally describes thin purées of vegetables, served as soup, as well as puréed seafood soups that would more accurately be named BISQUES. Occasionally, a fresh puréed vegetable sauce for meat or seafood—particularly one of tomatoes—will be so described.

COUSCOUS (ME)

The Arabic word for a fine-grained semolina pasta (the name derives from *rac keskes*, or crushed small) and for the elaborate main course based upon it. Traditionally, the semolina pasta is steamed over a fragrantly spiced stew of lamb or chicken and such typical vegetables as chick peas, onions, carrots and potatoes; raisins may also be included. The grain, cooked and flavored by the steam from the stew, is heaped on a platter, and the stew is spooned around it. A fiery chili sauce is passed separately for each guest to add to taste. Plain steamed couscous may also be eaten as a dessert, sprinkled with sugar, nuts and raisins.

à la CRÉCY (FR)

Synonymous with carrots, which grow fine and sweet in the northern French town of the same name. Croquettes of puréed carrot are *fondants Crécy; omelette à la Crécy* has a carrot filling; *purée Crécy* is cream of carrot soup; tiny puff pastries stuffed with carrot purée are *bouchées* (mouthfuls) *à la Crécy.*

CRÈME BRÛLÉE (FR/UK)

"Burnt cream" is a custard-cream dessert; "burnt" refers to the brittle, dark caramel crust on top of the thick, extremely rich vanilla cream. The dessert is made by spooning the custard into individual serving pots; a good layer of granulated sugar is sprinkled on top, and the pots are placed under a hot broiler until the sugar melts and darkens. (In centuries past, a red-hot poker was applied to the sugar to melt it.) The pots are then chilled, and the caramel sets hard. Each diner shatters the caramel with his spoon, eating pieces of it with the custard beneath. Oddly enough, the dish actually has dual nationality: recipes for burnt cream can be found in English cookbooks centuries old.

CRÈME CARAMEL (FR)

''Caramel cream'' describes a vanilla-flavored custard baked in a mold that has been coated with caramelized sugar syrup. The caramel dissolves to a thin sauce, which, when the custard is unmolded, runs down its side and surrounds it on the serving platter. So popular is this dessert that it is now as much a part of the cuisines of England, the United States and other countries—French name and all—as it is of France. In Spain and Latin America, the dessert is popular under the name FLAN.

CRÈME CHANTILLY (FR)

Named for a cream-producing suburb north of Paris. It is a sweetened whipped-cream dessert topping flavored with vanilla or a liqueur. When the crème is used as a pastry filling, the pastry takes on the name—as in a CHARLOTTE *à la Chantilly*.

CRÈME FRAÎCHE (FR)

Not really *fresh* cream, it is rather a heavy, slightly soured product, like a mixture of sour cream and heavy cream. *Nouvelle cuisine* has popularized it as a substitute for ordinary cream—an enrichment for soups, a sauce base for anything from pasta to veal or chicken, or an ingredient in fillings for such pastries as DACQUOISE. It makes a wonderful topping for fresh fruit, particularly berries.

CRÉOLE (US/FR)

A sauce popular with meats and chicken in the New Orleans kitchen, it is composed of tomatoes, peppers, onions, garlic and cayenne pepper. In France, a dish dressed with this sauce is known as *à la créole*. The designation may also indicate a garnish of rice with tomatoes and peppers.

CROQUEMBOUCHE (FR)

At once architecture and pastry, it is made from scores of tiny pastry balls piped full of a vanilla custard cream, sweetened whipped cream or some other rich filling. One by one the balls are dipped in molten caramel and stacked into a tall cone or pyramid shape, which is then decorated with a tracery of dribbled caramel. A portion of the structure is served to each diner. With every bite the hardened caramel goes "crunch" (*croque*) in the "mouth" (*bouche*). Croquembouches may also be made with orange segments or other small pieces of fruit, marzipan, tiny meringues or sponge cakes, all stuck together with caramel.

CRUMPETS (UK)

Incomparable griddle-cooked tea breads, about 4 inches in diameter, an inch or so thick and densely riddled with deep holes—the result of including baking soda as well as a yeast leaven and of beating the batter vigorously. Crumpets are toasted before serving. Their holes soak up butter like a sponge.

CSÍPETKE (EE)

Noodles made from an egg-and-flour dough pinched by hand into tiny pieces. Briefly boiled, they garnish GULYÁS and other stews and thick soups. Some natives claim tongue-in-cheek that they can tell just by eating the noodles whether they were made by a right- or left-handed cook.

CUISINE MINCEUR

See FRENCH COOKING.

CUISINE NOUVELLE

See FRENCH COOKING.

Good cookery is the food of a clear conscience.

—DES ESSARTS

DACQUOISE (FR)

Ground nuts—almonds and hazelnuts are the usual choices—are mixed with sugar and folded into beaten egg whites. The resulting meringue mixture may be spread into shallow circular pans or piped in spiraling circles; what matters is that two layers are formed and baked until golden, then left to cool. Between them goes a buttercream filling—flavored with mocha, vanilla, chocolate or some other complementary ingredient. The finished dacquoise, decorated with sifted sugar and served in wedges, offers contrasts of mellow and sweet flavors, and of crisp, chewy, smooth and crunchy textures.

DAIKON (JA)

A giant white radish, commonly a foot in length and anywhere from a few inches to a foot in diameter. It is an omnipresent Japanese vegetable, grated fresh and served as a salad with soy sauce, mixed into TEMPURA dipping sauce, braised in SUKIYAKI. Soaked in vinegar or soy sauce it also makes a delicate pickle.

DARNE (FR)

A thick fish steak, with bone, cut crosswise from a large fish—particularly salmon. It may be sautéed, grilled or braised.

DASHI (JA)

What good broth or consommé is to Western cooking, this is to Japanese. It is a simple soup, a cooking stock for such dishes as SUKIYAKI, and a sauce base for TEMPURA and the like. Clean and light in taste, it is the essence of dried kelp and flakes of dried bonito, briefly boiled and then strained.

DAUBE (FR)

The word means "mess," having the same root as the English "daub". It is a slightly offhand way of referring to a sublime, long-simmered stew—usually of beef, though sometimes of goose, lamb or pork. The meat is combined with a good stock, wine, carrots, onions, celery, turnips, a bundle of herbs and—for their suave, gelatinous quality—pork rinds and cubes of salt pork. The stew is cooked in a special earthenware pot, a *daubière*, with a wide bottom and a narrow neck to prevent evaporation. The lid is sealed on with a flour-and-water paste, and the daube cooks in a low oven for hours. It tastes best when it is then left to cool, skimmed of fat, and cooked an hour or two more. The traditional accompaniment is *macronade*, an oven-browned dish of noodles, butter and cheese, good for soaking up the sauce.

à la DAUPHINÉ (FR)

From the Dauphiné region, where potatoes are the favored vegetable, comes this GRATIN of mashed potatoes mixed with egg and an unsweetened CHOUX paste. Baked in a shallow dish, the thick, smooth mixture develops a tasty brown crust.

al DENTE (IT)

Italian for "to the tooth," it describes the optimum texture for well-cooked pasta or

47

vegetables. They should be tender, yet retain some "bite."

DEVILED

See *à la* DIABLE.

DHANSAK (IN)

The greatest dish of the Parsees, Indians of Persian descent. They first purée cooked lentils, blending the result with mixed vegetables such as eggplant, tomato, onion, squash and spinach, and a mild and subtle blend of spice fried in *ghee* (clarified butter), sautéed lamb or chicken, fresh green chili and coriander. Crisp fried onions go on top. Rich and luscious as the resulting feast is, it is easy to understand why the dish has its name: *Dhan* is Parsee for "wealth."

à la DIABLE (FR)

The word refers to meat—particularly chicken—that is grilled and breadcrumbed, then served with a diable sauce. The sauce, made with stock, white wine, vinegar, shallots and herbs, gets its devilish fire from cayenne pepper. Some versions may use mustard instead. Mustard becomes the rule when hardboiled eggs are deviled—that is, their yolks are mashed with piquant seasonings and stuffed back into the whites.

alla DIAVOLA (IT)

Often a preparation like the French *à la* DIABLE. More simply, it may refer to grilled meat—particularly chicken—seasoned with a devilish quantity of red or black pepper.

fra DIAVOLO

See FRA DIAVOLO.

DIJONNAISE (FR)

The mustard of Dijon, aromatic with the crushed grains of mustard seed and white-wine vinegar, flavors the sauce of any dish with this name—most often chicken or veal. The sauce may be finished with cream or with olive oil and egg.

DIM SUM (CH)

The name for these savory and sweet steamed, deep-fried or baked Chinese tea delicacies promises to "delight your heart." Served at breakfast in China, dim sum have become a popular luncheon speciality of many Western Chinese restaurants. In larger establishments, they are stacked in their baskets and plates atop rolling service carts; you select what you want as the cart passes by, and your bill is totaled from the number of empty containers left on your table.

Some notable dim sum: *bao,* fluffy rice-flour buns that may be stuffed with barbecued pork (*char siu*), chicken or sweet red-bean paste; tiny spareribs steamed in black-bean sauce; deep-fried finger-sized spring rolls filled with bean sprouts, and shrimp or pork; crisp wonton with a sweet-and-sour dipping sauce; squares of turnip paste flavored with dried shrimp; duck's feet steamed in a rich brown gravy; whole fresh shrimp deep-fried in edible rice-paper wrappers; *shiu mie,* mixtures of beef, pork or shrimp in delicate noodle wrappers; sticky fried-rice wrapped in an aromatic lotus leaf; firm cubes of coconut jelly; and small sweet egg-custard tartlets.

DOBOS TORTA (EE)

Seven thin, round sponge cakes are layered with chocolate cream—spread as thick or thicker than the cakes—to construct the high, round drum shape of this classic confection. The sides are spread with more chocolate cream, but the cake's most distinctive feature goes on top: a glaze of hot, golden caramel, scored into wedges while still molten to facilitate cutting after it sets.

DOLMATHES *or* **DOLMAS** (GR/ME)

Means simply "rolls." Since ancient times, Greek cooks have rolled up mixtures of rice and chopped meat in a variety of leaves: in the old days, fig and mulberry leaves were used; now grapevine and cabbage leaves are favored. Dolmathes are simmered in water and lemon juice and served cold, as an appetizer, or hot as a main course with AVGOLE-MONO sauce. Turkish *dolmades* are essentially

49

DU BARRY

similar, though the authentic ones are cooked in sheep's-tail fat.

DU BARRY (FR)

Madame du Barry, mistress of King Louis XV, is honored by a cauliflower garnish for meats. Florets of the vegetable are topped with MORNAY sauce and grated cheese, then cooked au GRATIN.

DUBLIN CODDLE (IR)

A Saturday night favorite in the Irish capital, this is a plain stew of onions, sausage and bacon simmered in water—the perfect combination for a palate marinated in drafts of whiskey and stout. In fact, stout is the ideal accompaniment to the coddle.

DUCHESSE potatoes (FR)

An elegant garnish for roast meats or poultry. Potatoes, puréed and mixed with egg yolks, are decoratively molded by hand or piped right on to the serving platter, then baked until golden.

à la DUGLÉRÉ (FR)

A style of cooking sole and other white-fleshed fish. The fish is poached in white wine with fish stock, butter, shallots and tomatoes. The dish was invented by the Parisian chef Adolphe Dugléré.

DUXELLES (FR)

A potent mixture of chopped mushrooms and shallots, cooked in butter and/or oil until almost dry. Duxelles was created in the seventeenth century by La Varenne, chef to the Marquis d'Uxelles. On its own or combined with other ingredients, duxelles lends flavor to stuffings for vegetables, crêpes, seafood, poultry and meats. Mushroom sauces are often made by adding duxelles to a BÉCHAMEL or a VELOUTÉ.

Faites simple. *Make it simple.*
—GEORGES AUGUSTE
ESCOFFIER

EASTERN EUROPEAN COOKING

The map of Europe has changed so drastically in the past century that it is difficult to draw culinary borders, especially for the recently juggled and re-formed countries of Eastern Europe. Similar dishes that in a large country might be classified as regional variations on a single theme are in Eastern Europe likely to be claimed as distinct national dishes: one need only consider BORSCH, whose ingredients and complexity vary more or less from country to country. Nevertheless, Eastern Europe comprises such a wide range of climates and terrains that, related though its cuisines may be, some distinctions can be found:

Bulgaria. Abutting Greece and Turkey as it does, this country has a decidedly Middle Eastern influence in its cooking. Indeed, Bulgaria was a part of the Ottoman Empire for more than 500 years. Its salads duplicate the Greek HORIATIKI. A delicious meat-and-vegetable casserole closely resembling MOUSSAKA and an abundance of yogurt dishes are also popular.

Czechoslovakia. A young country, cobbled together at the end of World War I, its cuisine is a blend of Germanic and Slavic influences. Hearty stews seasoned with caraway and moistened with cream are popular; among roast meats and poultry, the richness of pork, goose and duck is preferred. Dumplings are the staple accompaniment, and the quick lunch usually consists of sausages closely related to German WURST. A favorite dessert is sweet palachinky, a relative of the Hungarian PALACSINTA.

Hungary. GULYÁS springs immediately to mind, along with related paprika-laced stews such as PORKOLT and PAPRIKAS. These embody both the heartiness and the refinement characteristic of the Hungarian kitchen, and seen in other distinctive dishes such as the stuffed pancakes called PALACSINTA and the multi-layered cake known as DOBOS TORTA.

Poland. Honest country cooking is the keynote here, characterized by soups such as *barszcz* (see the Russian BORSCH)and CHLODNIK; by the national dish of sauerkraut and meats, called BIGOS; and by ZRAZY, stuffed cabbage. In true Eastern European style, dumplings, both savory and sweet, are the favorite starch.

Romania. The Turkish influence shows in rice- and meat-stuffed vegetables, dips of puréed eggplant with olive oil, and meat-and-vegetable casseroles with the familiar name *musaca*. A Hungarian sensibility also manifests itself, particularly in the addition of sour cream, lemon juice and peppers to dishes of braised meat or poultry.

Yugoslavia. Six disparate republics were united to form this country, and their styles of cooking differ just as their people do, with the influences of Austria, Hungary, Italy, Germany, Greece, Turkey and Russia all adding their strands to the cuisine's fabric. Nevertheless, yogurt is popular throughout the country, on its own, in salads and as an enrichment for sauces. Charcoal-grilled meats are commonplace. And the Yugoslav sweet tooth knows no boundaries, enjoying Hungarian sweet PALACSINTA as readily as Turkish BAKLAVA.

ÉMINCÉ (FR)

The French for "minced," this term describes any dish of meat or poultry—particularly leftovers—cut into small slivers or thin slices and gently heated in a sauce. Any sauce will do: a simple tomato sauce, a BORDELAISE, a CHASSEUR or a POIVRADE.

EMPANADA (LA/IB)

Though its name means "breaded" in Spanish, the empanada is in fact a pastry-enclosed, baked or fried turnover popular throughout Latin America, as well as in the Galician province of northwestern Spain. Fillings are highly seasoned mixtures of chopped meat, chicken, fish or vegetables. A standard empanada will be comparable in size to a sandwich, big enough to be a quick meal in itself; cocktail snack-sized ones are called by the diminutive, *empanaditas*.

ENCHILADA (MEX)

This is probably the most versatile TORTILLA-based dish of the Mexican kitchen. Tortillas are dipped in chili sauce, briefly fried, and rolled around a generous quantity of filling: shredded cheese, turkey or chicken, chunks of beef or pork, with any number of different chili sauces and other embellishments, from olives to scallions to almonds to bitter chocolate. Topped with more sauce and cheese, the enchiladas are heated briefly before serving. Sometimes, they are garnished with sour cream or GUACAMOLE.

ENOKI

See MUSHROOMS.

Eat not to dullness. Drink not to elevation.
—BENJAMIN FRANKLIN

FAGGOTS (UK)

The name comes from an old word meaning "bundles." In England's north, these are the quintessential country sausages. Made from an herbed mixture of ground offal, pork and breadcrumbs, they are shaped into compact square, round or loaf-shaped cakes and wrapped securely in caul fat (a thin, transparent sheet of fat) for baking. The faggots may be eaten hot or cold as a main dish for lunch or dinner.

FARFALE

See PASTA.

FEIJOADA (LA)

The national dish of Brazil, it shows the influences of Portugal, Mexico and Africa on the country's cuisine. It is a bounteous party dish of black beans (*feijão*) cooked with mixed meats, garlic, chilies and tomatoes. The meats are served sliced, moistened with the cooking juices, on a large platter: smoked beef-tongue at the center surrounded by fresh and dried beef; bacon; pigs' ears, feet and tails; and fresh and cured sausages. The beans are presented in a separate casserole, and the table is completed with rice, manioc meal, boiled kale or collard greens, a sauce of hot chili and lime and fresh orange segments.

FELAFEL (ME)

Deep-fried balls made of puréed chick peas, burghul (cracked wheat), garlic, cumin and other seasonings, they are served as a street food or a cocktail snack. In Israel, felafel is often tucked inside a PITA bread, with a TAHINI-and-pepper sauce and fresh salad; so popular is it in this form that it is jokingly called the Israeli hot dog.

à la FERMIÈRE (FR)

"In the style of the farmer's wife," this cooking method relies on meat pot-roasted in butter with farmhouse garden vegetables— carrots, turnips, celery and onions.

FETTUCCELLE

See PASTA.

FETTUCINE

see PASTA.

FILÉ (US)

A native American seasoning of powdered baby sassafras leaves. Filé gives its characteristic stickiness and spiciness to GUMBO and other Creole dishes.

à la FINANCIÈRE (FR)

Only a captain of finance, so it seems, is supposed to be able to afford this garnish for poultry, veal or sweetbreads, also used as a VOL-AU-VENT filling. The elitist ingredients are tiny QUENELLES of veal or chicken, cocks' combs and cocks' kidneys, mushrooms, olives and a JULIENNE of TRUFFLES. Sometimes truffles alone, simmered in Madeira, become a financière sauce.

FINES HERBES (FR)

A French term accepted into English for a mixture of chopped fresh parsley, chives, tarragon and chervil, in proportions of the cook's choice, whose flavors complement one another in a delicate bouquet. Most often they lend their accent to a tossed green salad or an *omelette aux fines herbes*.

FINNAN HADDIE (UK)

A Scottish pronunciation of "Findon haddock," haddock brought in at the fishing village of Findon, then split, gutted and smoked for about half a day. The fish's flesh takes on a mellow flavor and a deep amber color. Like a KIPPER, the fish may be buttered and grilled or poached, and it is usually served as a breakfast dish.

alla FIORENTINA (IT)

The Italian "in the style of Florence" is not to be confused with the spinach-oriented style indicated by the French term of the same meaning, *à la* FLORENTINE. In Italian, the term means simple, good-quality Tuscan cooking: roast saddle of pork (*arista*) with rosemary and garlic, for example; or steak (*bistecca*) charcoal-broiled with olive oil and served with fresh lemon; or tripe (*trippa*) braised with vegetables in stock and served with a dusting of Parmesan cheese.

FIRE POT (CH)

A main-course soup. The fire pot itself is a small charcoal brazier with a central chimney funnel, around which rests a ring-shaped basin filled with boiling broth. Platters of thin-sliced meat and vegetables are displayed around the pot at table. Each diner uses chopsticks to pick up pieces of food and

submerge them in the broth until cooked; then dips them into a sauce of seasame oil, pepper oil, soy sauce and rice wine and eats them. When all the food is gone, the enriched broth—sometimes supplemented with cellophane noodles—is ladled out and drunk as a soup. The exact contents of a fire pot vary with the region: The Mongolian version, perhaps the most famous, features only lamb or mutton as the meat, whereas a "chrysanthemum" fire pot from coastal Canton may include shrimp, sole, oysters and squid, along with chicken, calf's liver, pork and beef.

FIVE-SPICE POWDER (CH)

This classic Szechwan seasoning is a pulverized mixture of star anise, cinnamon, cloves, fennel and Szechwan peppercorns (red berries with a strong peppery taste). It lends its sweet and spicy flavor to many Chinese and other Asian dishes.

FLAMICHE (FR)

A specialty of Picardy on France's northwest coast, not far from Belgium, flamiche is undoubtedly Flemish in origin. A relative of the savory French tart, the quiche, now so familiar in English-speaking lands, it consists of a shortcrust tart casing filled with eggs and chopped, butter-stewed leeks.

FLAN (FR/IB/LA)

In its French version, this is nothing more than a superb example of what English speakers know as an open-faced pie or tart, filled with anything from custard to whipped cream to fresh or cooked fruits. In Spain and Latin America, the same word refers to a molded custard, particularly the dessert known elsewhere as CRÈME CARAMEL.

FLAUTAS (MEX)

The word means "flutes," and these tightly rolled TORTILLAS filled with meat, poultry or cheese mimic the form of the musical instrument. The rolls are deep-fried until crisp and are served as an hors d'oeuvre, a light lunch or a snack.

FLOATING ISLANDS
See *à la* NEIGE.

à la FLORENTINE (FR)
Always refers to spinach. When spinach first made its way into Italy from the Middle East during the Renaissance, it became a favorite of the wealthy Italian families like the Medicis of Florence. Though spinach in no way distinguishes true Florentine cooking today, the French give the city's name to many seafood and egg dishes served on a bed of spinach, covered with MORNAY sauce and grated cheese, and cooked *au* GRATIN. Any other sauté or stew into which spinach finds its way may also be so designated. The term should not be confused with the Italian designation *alla* FIORENTINA.

FOIE GRAS (FR)
The fattened liver of a goose or duck. If any one delicacy says *haute cuisine,* this specialty of Strasbourg and Toulouse is it. The words translate rather indelicately as "fat liver," meaning the liver of a goose (or, less often, duck) that is force-fed for six weeks with a warm porridge of cornmeal and fat, causing the bird's liver to swell. In effect, the goose becomes, as the French food writer C. Gérard put it, "a living hothouse in which grows the supreme fruit of gastronomy." At the age of ten months, the goose is killed. The fattened liver (over 2 pounds in weight) is firm; creamy in color with a pink blush; and has a rich, almost buttery flavor and consistency. It may simply be sliced, briefly sautéed in butter and served as a first course with a wine-and-butter sauce and with garnishes as humble as a bread crouton or as lavish as fresh black TRUFFLE. It may be baked in a BRIOCHE dough or poached and chilled in ASPIC, also as first courses. Foie gras is also the basis of, or a featured ingredient in, the most elegant PÂTÉS and TERRINES, and it is used as a garnish for sautéed meat and poultry courses in the more expensive restaurants. It also

makes a superb main course on its own, studded with pieces of truffle, then wrapped in a translucent sheet of caul fat and braised in stock and wine.

FONDUE (SW)

From the French *fondre,* meaning "to melt," comes the name for three different dishes, all of which make use of the fondue pot—a deep container perched atop an alcohol flame or other dinner-table heat source. Best known is cheese fondue, the *fondue Neuchâteloise:* Emmenthal, Gruyère, or a mixture of the two Swiss cheeses is gently melted with wine, garlic, kirsch and seasonings; each diner dips individual cubes of crusty bread, skewered on a long fork, into the molten cheese, then eats the cubes. For a beef fondue—also known as *fondue Bourguignonne* (because the Burgundy region once included Geneva, the Swiss capital)—the pot is filled with hot cooking oil, and each diner uses the fork to dip small pieces of fillet into the oil, cooking them to taste and then seasoning each mouthful with an array of sauces.

FONDUTA (IT)

A relative of Switzerland's cheese FONDUE. Like that dish, its name derives from the word "melt." It is made by melting Fontina cheese, similar to Emmenthal or Gruyère, with milk and egg yolks. The really distinctive feature comes at serving time: it is topped with fragrant shavings of white TRUFFLE.

FOOL (UK)

A centuries-old English dessert is made with a purée of cooked fruit. Tart green gooseberries are the definitive choice, though other fruits are frequently used. The fruit is blended with an equal amount of whipped cream or custard and served chilled. The name is an old usage, implying not stupidity but simplicity of preparation.

à la FORESTIÈRE (FR)

As a "forester" might prepare it, this style of cooking small pieces of meat or poultry teams them with woodland mushrooms, or morels, and with diced potato and bacon.

FRA DIAVOLO (IT)

"Brother Devil" was a seventeenth-century Italian monk who slipped away from his monastery to lead a life of crime. In his honor this devilish style of preparing lobster and other crustaceans was named. The shellfish are cut into pieces and sautéed in olive oil, then finished with a sauce of wine, tomatoes, onions, garlic, oregano, parsley and flakes of dried red pepper.

FRANKFURTERWURST

See WURSTS.

FRENCH COOKING

In terms of food, France is a nation uniquely blessed: seas to its west and south provide a bounteous catch of seafoods; rivers are full of trout and crayfish; pastures nurture dairy cattle; orchards are full of apples, gardens grow a variety of vegetables; vineyards overflow with grapes, wild mushrooms grow in the forests; sunny hillsides are perfumed with herbs and shaded by olive trees. And the French people have been blessed with the wisdom and ingenuity to transform these raw materials into great culinary creations. The best cooking of France is spread through all its regions. The following are some culinary high points of France's most notable provinces and of the country's top restaurant kitchens:

Alsace and Lorraine. Abutting Germany and historically connected to it, these provinces show the influence of that country's cooking. The sausages and hams are superb, and cabbage is the omnipresent vegetable. In the form of sauerkraut, it is joined with cured meats in the spectacular CHOUCROUTE *garnie;* with salt pork, fresh cabbage becomes the heartwarming soup POTÉE. Local bacon is also an essential element of the region's best-known exported recipe, *quiche Lorraine.* Nearby is the region called Champagne; there's no need to name its most famous product.

Bordeaux. Here in southwestern France some of the country's greatest wines are produced, and they lend their savor to the famous BORDE-LAISE sauce for the grilled meats favored in the region. Refined tastes are also catered to by such delicacies as the *cèpes* (see MUSHROOMS) growing wild in the region's woods; from Périgord come TRUFFLES and FOIE GRAS, which confer the name PÉRIGORDINE on many of the region's dishes.

Brittany. This is a land of simply cooked seafoods, hams and sausages. That all-purpose pancake wrapper, the crêpe, was invented here.

Burgundy. Burgundy's great wines bestow their name and character on many dishes, best known among which is the stew called *boeuf à la* BOURGUIGNONNE. The region's freshwater fish make excellent QUENELLES. The city of Dijon offers the gift of mustard, which often flavors dishes cooked *à la* DIJONNAISE. Neighboring Lyon makes lavish use of onions in its dishes prepared *à la* LYONNAISE.

Languedoc. The rich, substantial dishes of the region are epitomized in the casserole of meats and beans called CASSOULET. The region is also the home of the famous Roquefort cheese. To the southwest, in the foothills of the Pyrenees, can be found great Basque peasant dishes such as PIPÉRADE and GARBURE.

Normandy. Apples and cream, cider and the applejack brandy called Calvados create the distinctive character of the region's dishes—even combined with some of the fish caught along its coast in *la Manche,* also known as the English Channel.

Provence. The flavor here is assertively Mediterranean: tomatoes, garlic, onions, herbs such as basil and oregano, olives and olive oil, anchovies and fresh seafoods distinguish Provençal cooking. They are found in the vegetable stew called RATATOUILLE, and most famously in the BOUILLABAISE of Marseilles.

Haute Cuisine. According to the respected American food essayist M.F.K. Fisher, *haute cuisine* "may be one of modern man's nearest

61

approaches to pure bliss.'' It is a pleasure akin to that evoked by a symphony or a majestic work of classical architecture. Formality and elegance are essential: *haute,* after all, means "high." Only the finest materials are used: prime cuts of meat, blemish-free vegetables, the richest butter and cream, the finest wines, the most exquisite delicacies—TRUFFLES, FOIE GRAS, caviar (see ROES). The rules for preparing such refined ingredients were laid down in the nineteenth century by such great chefs as Marie-Antoine Carême and Auguste Escoffier; to this day, *haute cuisine* is not so much a creative art as a matter of following well-established formulas for cooking and presenting the classic dishes. Say *tournedos* ROSSINI to an *haute cuisine* chef and he will know precisely how to prepare and arrange these fillet steaks with *foie gras* and truffles. Ask him to prepare a sauce BÉARNAISE and he will know the exact proportions of egg yolks, vinegar and FINES HERBES. In fact, he will have memorized recipes for hundreds of rich sauces in the *haute cuisine* repertoire; scores of specially named consommés with their colorful and delicate embellishments; countless garnishes of carefully prepared vegetables; decorations of jewellike ASPIC; and a selection of suave CHAUD-FROID glazes that give impeccable beauty to every platter that leaves his kitchen. This elaborate perfection is seen in *haute cuisine's* desserts and pastries as well—including the regal *riz à l'* IMPÉRATRICE; the light, flaky, cream-filled MILLE-FEUILLE; and the layered meringue-and-buttercream dessert known as DACQUOISE.

Nouvelle Cuisine. Literally "new cookery," this refers to the current phase in the evolution of French cuisine, pioneered by the late Fernand Point and his disciples, among them Paul Bocuse and Michel Guérard. With an emphasis on absolutely fresh, top-quality ingredients, prepared and presented elegantly and simply, *nouvelle cuisine* rejects *haute cuisine's* dishes laden with egg yolks and cream, its flour-thickened sauces and its elaborate preparations.

Nouvelle cuisine dishes tend to be under-cooked. Flesh is served rare, be it lamb, duck or even sometimes fish; vegetables come *al* DENTE. Sauces are light, often just reductions of pan juices deglazed with a touch of wine, a squeeze of citrus juice, or some unusual vinegar scented with berries or herbs—and, well, maybe just a little butter or cream too.

Within these precepts, there is a lot of room for a chef to exercise his originality and imagination. You'll sometimes find unusual combinations of meats, vegetables, fruits and seasonings—rare FOIE GRAS with raspberries, for example, or lobster with mint. But bizarre for bizarre's sake is not *nouvelle*. The overall sensibility of good cooking must still reign supreme, as is evident in such already-classic *nouvelle* dishes as rare duck breast with green peppercorns, layered TERRINES of fresh vegetables and FOIE GRAS PÂTÉ, and poached whole peaches on a bed of red wine sorbet.

Cuisine Minceur. What *nouvelle cuisine* is to *haute, minceur* is to *nouvelle*. The three-star chef Michel Guérard devised this elegant "slimmer's cooking" in an effort to get rid of the weight he himself had put on in his rise to culinary fame. He eliminated all sugars and fats from his cooking, steaming fish and poultry, roasting only lean meats, dressing salads with vinegar or lemon, preparing unsweetened sorbets of good ripe fruits. His presentation is exquisite, but sparing. Beautiful, tasteful and tasty though *cuisine minceur* may be, however, diet food it remains.

FRIJOLES REFRITOS (MEX)

"Refried beans" are really fried only once. Dried red beans are cooked until tender, with onions, garlic, chilies and sometimes tomatoes. Then they are coarsely mashed and fried slowly in lard until they become a good, thick paste. Garnished with shredded cheese, the beans are a standard side dish with most Mexican meals, as well as being an ingredient in such TORTILLA assemblies as

TOSTADAS and QUESADILLAS. *Refrito* means "well-fried," not "twice-fried".

FRIKADELLER (SC)

Denmark's popular ground-meat dish is a cross between hamburgers and meatloaf—a canny way of stretching the meat that costs so much there. A mixture of finely ground meats—veal and pork are the most frequent choices—is combined with breadcrumbs, onion, egg, milk and seasonings. The light smooth paste that results is shaped into small patties and sautéed in butter and oil until well browned. Frikadeller are served hot with pickled beets or cucumbers.

FRITTATA (IT)

This thick, pancakelike omelet is more vegetable than it is egg. A few of the latter are included simply as a binder for an abundance of chopped cooked spinach, shredded zucchini, chopped and sautéed mushrooms or the like. The mixture is poured into a hot pan liberally coated with olive oil, or oil and butter, and cooked until browned and set; then it is turned over and cooked until the other side is done. The omelet may be served hot, tepid or cold—cut in wedges as an hors d'oeuvre or presented whole as a light luncheon course.

FUL MEDAMMES (ME)

Egypt's national dish, a true dish of the people. Small, purplish dried broad beans are stewed with lentils in water. When tender, they are mashed together with olive oil, lemon juice and sometimes garlic, and eaten garnished with chopped egg. The dish is popular at breakfast, but street vendors sell the beans all day. They are also offered at even the finest Cairo restaurants.

FUSILLI

See PASTA.

All things that are green should have a little crispness, for if they are over-boiled, they neither have any sweetness or beauty.
    —HANNAH GLASSE

GADO-GADO (SEA)

If countries were to have national salads, this would be Indonesia's. It is assembled from whatever vegetables are at hand: string beans, carrots, cabbage and cauliflower, cut up and cooked *al* DENTE; diced and boiled potatoes; and raw lettuce, spinach, bean sprouts and cucumbers. Garnishes include fried or raw bean curd (TOFU), sliced hard-boiled eggs and crisp fried onions. Grand though this combination is, gado-gado's real glory is its dressing, poured hot over the salad just before serving—a sweet, spicy, mellow mixture of peanut butter, sugar, chilies and coconut milk.

GALANTINE (FR)

From the old French *galine,* meaning "chicken." it is a PÂTÉ-like creation made from a whole boned chicken. The chicken is stuffed with an herbed and truffled mixture of minced veal and pork, then sewn up, wrapped in muslin and poached in gelatinous

65

stock and wine. The stuffed roll is then un-wrapped and left to cool, and its cooking liquid sets into ASPIC. The galantine and its aspic are served, in slices as a grand luncheon course or as an hors d'oeuvre. Nowadays, casings other than chicken may be used, in which case the type of casing will become part of the dish's name: galantine of veal or galantine of pheasant, for example.

GARBURE (FR)

The abundant main course from Béarn in the Pyrenees starts with a cauldron of violently boiling water. The best cooks specify that the pot must never stop boiling while the dish cooks. In go chunks of potato; next come fresh beans and peas, and, in the autumn, roasted chestnuts; then a huge bundle of thyme, parsley and marjoram, with garlic and seasonings; and finally chopped or shredded cabbage. The order is important, to ensure that each vegetable is done to a turn. When the last vegetable is done, a hunk of pre-served meat—sausage, ham, or goose, with its luscious rendered fat—is heated in the soup. A spoon will stand up in a well-made pot of garbure. The meat may be served on the side or in the soup, and the soup itself is ladled into serving bowls over dried crusts of bread. Garbure is accompanied by red wine, and a custom demands that each diner add the last gulp of his glass to the last few spoonfuls of soup in his bowl. This last mixture, called a *goudale*, is the Béarnaise equivalent of our "apple a day," supposed to ward off doctors.

GAZPACHO (IB)

From the southern region of Andalusia comes this thick, cold soup of fresh tomatoes, garlic, sweet peppers, olive oil, vinegar, salt and breadcrumbs. Gazpacho is presented together with an array of garnishes: croutons, chopped egg, tomatoes, onion, cucumber and peppers. Other provinces have their own variations, from the white, almond-based gazpacho of Málaga to a hot version with beans served in Cádiz.

GEFILTE FISH (JE)

Gefült is German for "stuffed." Originally the dish was made by stuffing a filleted fish with a mixture of chopped white fish, eggs, onions and seasonings (pike is the preferred). Nowadays gefilte fish is the filling mixture alone, molded into oblong cakes or larger loafs, then poached or baked. It may be eaten hot or cold, as an appetizer or a light main course, dipped into grated horseradish, which is often colored red with beet juice.

GÉNOISE (FR)

The famous French spongecake evolved in the early eighteenth century from a recipe that had originated in Genoa, Italy. The cake gets its lightness from whisked eggs, its richness from melted butter. Génoises are usually baked in round pans; when done, the cakes are halved horizontally, filled with apricot jam or a buttercream and coated with frosting.

alla GENOVESE (IT)

In Genoa, on Italy's northwest coast, herbs are the predominant seasoning—fresh basil in particular. The aromatic basil sauce called PESTO is a specialty of the city, and when it dresses GNOCCHI or seasons minestrone, the famous chunky vegetable soup, the alla genovese label is applied.

GERMAN AND AUSTRIAN COOKING

Hearty, filling fare is what comes to mind when Germanic cooking is mentioned. Germans and Austrians love to eat.

Germans, tradition has it, consume five meals a day: bread and coffee for breakfast; a light mid-morning meal such as cold cuts, cheeses and bread; a large cooked lunch; afternoon coffee and pastries; and an evening meal of sausages, salads, bread and beer. German sausages are superb, and they come in a great many varieties (see WURSTS). Germans love all kinds of meats; indeed, according to an old Bavarian saying, "meat is the best vegetable." Roasts and braises and stews abound, flavored with surprisingly complex combinations of herbs and spices: consider the famous, subtly sweet-and-sour pot roast, SAUERBRATEN, or the peppery hare stew, HASENPFEFFER. Accompanying the main course are likely to be braised red cabbage or green cabbage, the latter often in the form of sauerkraut; boiled potatoes; and a prodigious procession of dumplings, some huge and hefty, others (like SPATZEL) appealingly delicate—but still filling.

Austrian cooking tends to be somewhat lighter than German cooking and far more eclectic, showing in particular the influences of the Hungarian and Czech kitchens (see EASTERN EUROPEAN COOKING). Vienna, the capital, has given the world the most famous version of the *schnitzel* (meat cutlet), the WIENERSCHNITZEL. But its truest fame lies in its cakes and pastries: SACHERTORTE, GUGEL-HUPF, LINZERTORTE and a dazzling array of other creations fill the tables of the cafés for which Vienna is so renowned.

GIARDINIERA (IT)

When prefixed by *alla,* it means "gardener's style," a garnish of mixed fresh vegetables for meats, poultry, fish or pasta. There is also a Milanese specialty known by the name *giardiniera di sottaceti* (roughly, "vinegared vegetables"), a combination of onions, peppers, string beans and kidney beans, carrots and celery cooked and served cold in vinegar as an ANTIPASTO.

GIROLLES

See MUSHROOMS.

GLASSBLOWER'S HERRING

See HERRINGS.

GNOCCHI (IT)

Dumplings that serve as a popular alternative to pasta. They have a reassuring wholesomeness and simplicity: the name is slang for "dullard." A cooked paste of semolina, farina or mashed potato and flour is cooled and shaped into small rounds, balls or short cylinders. The mixture may also include cheese or, for *gnocchi verdi*, spinach.

GOHANMONO

See JAPANESE COOKING.

GOLDEN CAVIAR

See ROES.

GOUGÈRE (FR)

Choux pastry is the basis of this savory hors d'oeuvre. The unbaked dough is mixed with grated cheese—Cheddar, Gruyère and Parmesan are all appropriate—and then piped or spooned onto a baking sheet either as small individual balls or as connected larger balls or mounds forming a ring. Baked, the pastry puffs up and browns and the cheese blends with the eggs and butter for a satisfying, mellow flavor.

GOULASH

See GULYÁS.

GRAMIGNA

See PASTA.

GRAND VENEUR Sauce (FR)

The words mean "big huntsman," referring to the master of the hunt. The sauce dresses venison and other fresh game. Based on a flour-thickened POIVRADE sauce made with game broth, it includes wine, vinegar, herbs, cream and red-currant jelly.

GRANITA (IT)

A Neapolitan dessert of finely shaved ice (the name refers to the slightly grainy texture) combined with an intensely flavored syrup—espresso, coffee, crushed strawberries, citrus juice and red wine are some popular choices. *Granite* (the plural) were first popularized in the eighteenth century by the café owner Tortoni, who gave his name to the famous frozen dessert BISCUIT TORTONI.

GRATIN (FR)

French for "crust," the word refers to any dish with a browned or crusty topping of breadcrumbs, cheese or a creamy sauce such as BÉCHAMEL. There are gratins of crayfish tails in cream sauce; gratins of shredded vegetables in butter, topped with breadcrumbs and cheese; and even dessert gratins, such as mandarin oranges cloaked in a SABAYON lightly browned under the broiler.

GRAVLAX (SC)

Gravad lax is an alternative spelling, and the words are Swedish for "buried salmon." Originally, this cured fish appetizer was actually weighted with earth. Today, two filleted sides of salmon are coated with fresh dill, sugar, salt and pepper, sandwiched together and pressed under boards and weights for several days, until the fish is firm and imbued with the flavorings. Sliced on the bias, the salmon is served with a sweet mustard-and-dill sauce.

à la GRECQUE (FR)

"Greek style" is how the French see this method of preparing one or several vegetables as an hors d'oeuvre or salad. Mushrooms, zucchini, small onions, artichoke hearts and other vegetables are briefly simmered with white wine, water, vinegar, olive

oil, lemon juice, oregano, thyme, bay, coriander seeds and peppercorns—a combination with a decidedly Mediterranean flair. The vegetables are then left to cool in this aromatic liquid and may be refrigerated in it for several days, acquiring a sharp, lightly pickled flavor.

GREMOLATA (IT)

A vibrant seasoning and a colorful garnish, it combines chopped garlic, parsley and grated orange and lemon peel. Although it may turn up in a stuffing or sprinkled over any braise, its preeminent role is to add the final burst of flavor to the Milanese speciality *osso buco* just before serving.

GRIBICHE (FR)

A smooth, piquant sauce for cold fish, made by mashing hardboiled egg yolks with oil and vinegar, chopped gherkins, capers and FINES HERBES.

GROENE HARING

See HERRINGS.

GUACAMOLE (MEX)

A dip, a salad or a garnish, guacamole is made by puréeing (or chopping) ripe avocadoes with roasted chilies, onion and lemon juice. The recipe varies all over the country, and other occasional additions are olive oil, cilantro, cumin, chopped tomatoes and shredded cheese. (American versions from the Tex-Mex and California kitchens often include sour cream.) Scooped up with TORTILLA chips, it is an excellent appetizer or snack; it can also be served on a bed of lettuce and eaten as a salad. A dollop of guacamole will sometimes adorn a TACO, ENCHILADA, TOSTADA or other Mexican main course.

GUGELHUPF *or* KUGELHOPF (AU)

The classic Viennese coffee cake, made from a rich egg sponge or yeast dough, baked in a deep, fluted ring mold and dusted with sugar. Often, the dough is layered in the mold with a sweetened poppyseed filling or chopped nuts; sometimes a marbled effect is created with a contrasting chocolate dough. Emperor Franz Josef I was wooed with small gugelhupf baked by his mistress, the Viennese actress Katharina Schatt.

GULYÁS (EE)

A beef stew, it is Hungary's most famous dish, and its fame has led to a worldwide misunderstanding. It is a paprika-flavored stew or thick soup, but paprika alone does not define the dish, as it does the putative goulash often found in the West. It is really a rustic, peasant concoction (the name means "shepherd's stew") made from cubed beef cooked with chopped onion and diced potato and liberally laced with the russet-toned, fiery paprika as well as with whole caraway seeds; other possible, but not essential, additions are peppers, garlic and tomato. Only in one authentic version is sour cream used: the *Székelygulyás* of Transylvania, which also includes sauerkraut. The stew is served with tiny noodles such as CSÍPETKE.

GUMBO (US)

The name comes from *gombos*, the Congolese word for "okra," and this soup-stew from Louisiana is indeed brimming with that vegetable, which gives it a characteristic gelatinous consistency. Some kind of smoked meat is always included, whether ham hocks, smoked duck or even spicy sausage. The abundant Gulf seafoods are a natural addition: Shrimp, oysters and crab all make regular appearances. The huntsman's bag is naturally emptied in as well: Down-home versions may include wild duck, rabbit or squirrel. More conventional meats—veal, beef, pork or chicken—are also fitting. Simmered for several hours with tomatoes, peppers, onions, garlic, fresh herbs, Tabasco pepper sauce, and FILÉ powder, gumbo is as rich and exciting a dish as the South has to offer. Thin versions are served as first-course soups; thicker gumbo is served as a main dish.

H

A nation's prosperity is measured not by the number of its inhabitants, but by the quantity of food at their disposition.
—HAN FEI-TSE

HAMS

About a third of all pork is cured in some way; the hindquarters of the pig that most often become hams. Coated with sugars, salt and seasonings, injected with or immersed in brines, air-dried, smoked over fragrant wood, aged for up to a year: The range and combination of treatments practiced all over the world results in hams with a wide spectrum of tastes and textures, some that require cooking and remain perishable, others so well preserved that they may be eaten raw and will keep for years.

Bayonne (FR). Most of these famous *jambons* are produced not in the Basque city of that name but in the Béarnaise town of Orthez—using salt from Bayonne. Smoked at low temperatures over a long period of time, the ham develops a dark honey color and mildly smoky flavor. It is eaten raw, thinly sliced, as an hors d'oeuvre; it is also often added to egg dishes.

Bradenham (UK). From Wiltshire, this sweet cooking ham derives its flavor from the molasses and juniper berries rubbed into it during six months of curing. It has a distinctive black rind.

Campagne (FR). Not one specific ham, this term refers to all the hams of the French countryside, varying in their qualities from region to region, town to town. In some places, the ham is cooked, in others, eaten raw; some hams may be heavily smoked, others mildly or not at all.

Lachsschinken (GE). It means "salmon ham," a good description for the color and texture of this smoked loin of pork (a departure from the usual cut for hams), thinly sliced and eaten raw as an hors d'oeuvre.

Parma (IT). See prosciutto below.

Pragerschinken (EE). This Czech ham, from Prague, is famous as a hot or cold main course, cooked whole. It has a mildly salty and sweet flavor, the result of several months of brine-curing followed by beechwood-smoking.

Prosciutto (IT). The famous ham of Parma is dry-salted for a month, then hung in huge curing sheds where the cool air of the northern Italian hills dries it over the course of half a year. The ham is best eaten raw, cut into tissue-thin slices that show off its dark pink color; it also finds its way into stuffings and creamy pasta sauces.

Serrano (IB). This is Spain's answer to prosciutto, similar in flavor but tending to be somewhat tougher, being made from pigs less pampered—and therefore more muscular—than their Parman cousins.

Smithfield (US). These are made from Virginia porkers, fed on peanuts and corn to plump up and sweeten their flesh. After a peppery dry-salt cure, they are smoked with apple and hickory wood, then aged for over a year. Though they could be eaten raw, the hams are usually boiled or glazed and baked. The meat's savory sweetness won the heart of Queen Victoria, who had a standing order for half-a-dozen hams per week.

Westphalian (GE). The hindquarters of acorn-fed pigs are briefly dry-salted, then brined and finally smoked with beechwood and juniper. Almost mahogany in color, the ham has a mellow, smoky flavor; it is delicious raw in thin slices, though it may also be boiled whole.

York (UK). Cured with dry salt, aged for several months and then smoked, it is considered a top-class cooking ham. York hams are now made all over the world, but not in York—the style of curing and smoking merely originated there. Depending on where it was made, the ham may range from a light to an intense smoky flavor.

HANOI SOUP (SEA)

One of Vietnam's most famous dishes, it is a full-meal soup of oxtail, beef, rice sticks, vegetables and a bold bouquet of seasonings that includes ginger, star anise, fresh coriander and the salted fish sauce called NUOC MAM. In Vietnam, it is served for breakfast, and many restaurants there specialize in it; in the West, it has become a first course or entrée for lunch or dinner. Both at home and abroad, its presentation is ceremonious: The cooked rice sticks are first heaped into bowls; boiled beef and oxtail meat go on top; then come thin raw-beef slices, which are lightly cooked when the broth is poured over them. Each diner garnishes his serving with bean sprouts, onions, fresh lime, fresh hot chilies and extra *nuoc mam*.

HASENPFEFFER (GE)

The words for "hare" and "black pepper" make up the name and the stew it refers to, a country specialty cooked in stock and red wine with onions and herbs. Aside from its distinctive peppery flavor, the stew is also sometimes seasoned with lemon juice and, to lend it a smoother flavor and consistency, a touch of bitter chocolate.

HAUTE CUISINE

See FRENCH COOKING.

HÉLÈNE (FR)

The name affixed to a classic pear dessert. The pears are peeled, poached whole in vanilla syrup, cooled and placed on top of vanilla ice cream, then drizzled with hot chocolate sauce just before serving.

HENRI IV (FR)

The sixteenth-century French king was the first to wish for "a chicken in every pot" for his subjects but is honored in culinary circles with this garnish for sautéed veal or beef. It consists of potato balls browned in butter, artichoke hearts filled with BÉARNAISE sauce (named after the region in which Henri was born) and strips of TRUFFLE. Hearty rather than prissy, the garnish accords well with the popular flair of the king whose grandfather had baptized him at birth with a crushed clove of garlic and a dash of wine applied to his lips.

HERRINGS

"Of all the fish that swim in the sea, the herring it is the fish for me," says an old Scottish shanty. These rich-flavored, oily fish have been prized in Europe for centuries. Because of their high oil content and the fact that their strong flavor stands up well to smoke, salt and other pickling ingredients, herrings are prime candidates for preserving. Many different cuisines offer their own variations. In Holland and Scandinavia, they are also enjoyed so briefly salted that they are virtually raw. Without even considering the hundreds of recipes for cooking the fish, here are some of the major varieties of herrings:

Bismarck (GE). A fresh herring is boned and marinated for a day in vinegar scented with onions, chilies and juniper berries.

Bloater (UK). Left whole and ungutted, these are briefly salted and then lightly smoked. The English grill the ever-so-slightly gamey fish with butter or make a paste from them that is used as a sandwich spread.

Bornholmer (SC). The small Baltic herring, caught off the Danish island of Bornholm, is in one day netted, gutted and hot-smoked over alderwood. The juicy, aromatic flesh is enjoyed in fillets with buttered rye-bread.

Bouffi (FR). The Gallic version of the Bloater.

Buckling (UK/BNL). An English and Dutch favorite: whole fish are gutted, briefly salted, then smoked over a hot fire that also cooks them. They are eaten cold as a first or light main course, with lemon and horseradish sauce.

Glassblower's (SC). The most famous of Sweden's many marinated herring dishes: sliced, salted herring fillets are layered in a tall glass jar (hence the name) with onions, carrots, horseradish and bay leaves, then submerged for several days in a sweetened vinegar marinade.

Groene *or* **"Green"** (BNL). Dutch for *Matjes.*

Kipper (UK). It is so prominent it merits its own entry. See KIPPER.

Matjes (GE). Means "little girls," an affectionate name for these immature herrings, caught in May, filleted and lightly cured in a salt-and-sugar brine. Chopped raw onion is the classic accompaniment for Matjes herring.

Rollmops (GE). Made from fillets rolled up around sliced onions and gherkins, secured with a toothpick and pickled for a week or more in a spiced vinegar brine.

HOISIN (CH)

A savory-sweet, syruplike dark brown sauce made from soybeans and used as a table condiment for meat, poultry or seafood. Its best-known use is as a dressing inside the pancake wrappers for PEKING DUCK.

HOLLANDAISE (FR)

It enjoys a reputation as the most exquisite of sauces—for eggs, vegetables or seafood.

Hollandaise is an emulsion of egg yolks and fat, with butter whisked in bit by bit over gentle heat. Seasoned with lemon juice, salt and white pepper, and finished perhaps with a touch of cream, the sauce is served warm.

HOPPER (IN)

A speciality of Sri Lanka (Ceylon), this bread or first course consists of a crisp, deep-fried pancake shaped like a large cup, made from a batter of rice flour and coconut milk. When served at the start of a meal, it often has a lightly poached or fried egg inside. The egg and pancake are eaten together, each mouthful spiked with a spicy CHUTNEY.

HOT AND SOUR SOUP (CH)

Suan la tang to the people of Szechwan province, this thick soup gets its heat from pepper and red chili and its sourness from white vinegar. These combine with a base of chicken stock, seasoned with soy sauce and sesame oil, crammed full of shredded roast pork and duck, Chinese mushrooms and cloud ear fungus (see MUSHROOMS), TOFU, bamboo shoots—and topped with a sprinkling of chopped, fresh scallion greens.

HUMMUS (ME)

A purée of boiled chick peas (garbanzo beans), TAHINI, garlic, lemon juice and seasonings. It is a popular appetizer throughout the Middle East—in Greece and Turkey, Israel and the Arab states alike. It is served with pieces of hot PITA bread, which are dipped into the hummus.

HUNANESE COOKING

See CHINESE COOKING.

HUNDRED-YEAR EGGS

See THOUSAND-YEAR EGGS.

HUSH PUPPIES (US)

A Southern specialty, these are deep-fried balls of onion-flavored cornmeal batter served with fried fish. The name has a simple explanation: At big open-air fish fries, cooks tossed extra portions of the fritters to the dogs to hush their noisy begging.

*The whole of nature, as has been
said, is a conjugation of the verb to
eat, in the active and passive.*
—WILLIAM RALPH INGE

IBERIAN COOKING

Spain and Portugal have distinct but related cuisines. In both countries the olive tree thrives: its first is a popular hors d'oeuvre or garnish, and the oil extracted from the fruit is the omnipresent cooking medium.

Portugal. Fronting the Atlantic, Portugal has a cuisine that emphasizes seafoods, both fresh and, in the form of *bacalhau* (see BACALAO), preserved. The cooking is simple, seasoned with herbs (particularly coriander), garlic, vinegar and lemon juice; tomatoes, onions and pimientos add their character to soups and stews.

Spain. A number of Spain's specialties feature seafood: the ZARZUELA of Catalonia in the northwest, for example, and the versions of PAELLA served along the country's southeast, Mediterranean coast. Olive oil, garlic, onions, tomatoes and peppers are constant notes in the cuisine; they harmonize memorably in the cold Andalusian soup GAZPACHO. Stews of meats, poultry, game and sausages (including the notable CHORIZO) have an honest country generosity: the centuries-old *co-cido* of Madrid and its Catalonian relative, the OLLA PODRIDA, are not just main courses but complete meals. This generosity can also be seen in Madrid's idea of bar snacks, the overwhelming array called *tapas*.

à l'IMPÉRATRICE (FR)

Many dishes were named in honor of the Empress of France, Eugénie, wife of Napoleon III. But the one that survives to this day is a molded rice pudding, *riz à l'impératrice*. It is a regal mixture of rice and abundant candied fruits, bound together in vanilla custard and spiked with kirsch.

à l'IMPÉRIALE (FR)

Imperial tastes, so this classic garnish combination for meats and poultry would have us believe, tend toward the expensive and the very refined: black TRUFFLES, FOIE GRAS and cocks' combs and kidneys.

INDIAN COOKING

It is a shame that the musty, denatured curries so often served in Western, non-Indian restaurants should shape people's attitudes toward the cuisine—or more correctly, cuisines—of the Indian subcontinent. There is no one such sauce as "curry": every Indian dish has its own subtle blend of spices, herbs and other flavorings—cumin and cinnamon, fennel and coriander, cloves and cardamom, saffron and mustard, turmeric and nutmeg, garlic and ginger, chilies and mint and coconut and tamarind. The country's kitchens have so many different dishes to offer:

Northern India's best-known specialty is TANDOORI cooking, named after the unusual oven that produces succulent, lightly charred, subtly spiced meats, particularly chicken and the region's omnipresent lamb. Popular, too, are PILAF-like BIRIANIS and a wide array of imaginatively shaped breads such as NAAN, PARATHA and CHAPATI.

Western Indian cooking features such rich dishes as the Parsee DHANSAK and the foods of

Goa, which are tempered by the influence of its Portuguese past.

Southern Indian food features with vegetarian dishes, although the practice of vegetarianism is followed by many devout Hindus throughout the country. Proteins come from dried beans and lentils, and the seasoning is far spicier— epitomized by the region's premier nonvegetarian preparation, VINDALOO. The island of Sri Lanka, off the southern coast, practices an even more fiery cuisine, although it is also known for a mild treat of an hors d'oeuvre, the HOPPER.

Bangladesh, a Muslim nation to the east of India, favors seafoods liberally spiced with mustards and chilies.

Pakistan, also Muslim and to the west of the subcontinent, shows some Middle Eastern influence, with many KABABS and other grilled meats as well as the liberal use of yogurt—though all these dishes are also popular within India. Many other Pakistani dishes are indistinguishable from those of northern India.

INDIAN PUDDING (US)

A mush of cornmeal, milk, molasses and perhaps eggs, cream, sugar, butter, cinnamon or ginger. This wholesome, satisfying dessert was invented by the Pilgrim colonists of New England. They called corn Indian corn—hence, the name.

INVOLTINI (IT)

These "little packages" consist of veal (or sometimes beef or chicken) rolled around a filling, be it ham, cheese, chicken livers or an herbed breadcrumb mixture. Dusted with flour, browned in butter or oil, and braised in stock and wine, the little rolls are served with their braising liquid boiled down to a syrupy and suave sauce.

ITALIAN COOKING

Italians can justifiably lay claim to having been the true inventors of French cooking. In 1533, Catherine de' Medici of Florence came to France to marry the man who would later become King Henri II. She brought with her a brigade of fine Italian chefs, who changed the cooking and eating habits of the aristocracy and ultimately, of the nation. Granted, it seems that two main elements of the Italian kitchen never really made the transfer to France: PASTA, in all its many forms, and RISOTTO, the rich, soupy rice dish that in the north of the country surpasses even pasta in popularity. But in the Italian *antipasti* we can see the origin of French hors d'oeuvres; in Italy's many pan-fried, garnished dishes we can see France's sautées; and clearly Italy's cakes and pastries were inspiration to the French art of *pâtisserie*. Working from north to south, here are some features of the key Italian cities and their regions:

Turin and the Piedmont. In this northeastern corner of the country, cooking is basic and hearty. It is also lavish, not surprising in the region where white TRUFFLES are found. This delicacy scents two of the region's most renowned specialties, the hot dip for vegetables known as BAGNA CAUDA and the melted cheese dish called FONDUTA. The Fontina cheese used in the latter dish also appears in local versions of the cornmeal-based POLENTA and the dumplinglike cousins of pasta, GNOCCHI. And Piedmontese generosity is epitomized in its main course of mixed boiled meats, BOLLITO MISTO.

Genoa and Liguria. Seafood is a mainstay on the northwest coast—simmered in soups or sautéed or deep-fried in the region's beloved olive oil. Herbs abound here—particularly fresh basil, which goes into Genoa's finest culinary creation, PESTO, a sauce that graces pastas and the local versions of minestrone soup and GNOCCHI.

Milan and Lombardy. Rice is king in the northern city of Milan: The city's version of *risotto* reigns supreme. It accompanies OSSO BUCO, the famed aromatic braise of veal shank, which along with Lombardy's meat-based version of *frito misto*, typifies the abundant cooking of the region. *Polenta* is also popular here. Milan's abundance is also evident in its confections, especially the world-renowned Christmas cake PANETTONE.

Venice and the Veneto. Seafood is prominent in the cooking of the northeastern city of canals: scampi, shrimp, eels, mussels, mullet and sole are among the many fish and shellfish harvested in the Gulf of Venice. They appear in the city's versions of RISOTTO; in soups; and, in the case of scampi, bathed in garlic butter. A light-colored, fine-textured variety of POLENTA is enjoyed in the Veneto. Further north, in the Italian Dolomite mountains, the cooking shows an Austro-Hungarian influence, with plenty of cured meats and even a local version of GULYÁS.

Bologna and Emilia-Romagna. The people of this region are great eaters. They enjoy a diet rich in pork—they even cook with lard rather than oil or butter. As the capital city's name might imply, famous pork sausages come from Bologna—particularly the variety known as MORTADELLA. Another notable cured meat of the region is the prosciutto of Parma (see HAMS). Chopped fresh pork, simmered for hours with tomatoes and herbs, produces Bologna's preeminent pasta sauce, RAGÙ, which graces the ribbon-shaped tagliatelle noodles favored here.

Florence and Tuscany. Farther south, olive oil begins to come into its own, gracing a simple cuisine that, inland, favors beef and *fagioli*, or haricot beans. Florentine cooking likewise follows a simple course, but, contrary to the French term *à la* FLORENTINE, *la cucina* FIORENTINA does not feature spinach at every turn. Along the coast, good, simple seafood dishes are prepared—a fine example of which is the fish stew called *cacciucco alla* LIVORNESE.

Rome and Latium. The capital naturally is a showcase for the best cooking of all Italy's regions. Its own specialties and those of its surrounding regions are characterized not so much by specific ingredients as by heartiness and simplicity: grand roasts of meat, particularly whole suckling pig or lamb, scented with the favorite herbs of the area, mint and rosemary; light sautées such as the veal SALTIMBOCCA; uncomplicated but vibrant-tasting treatments for PASTA such as *all'* ALFREDO, *alla* CARBONARA, *all'* AMATRICIANA.

Naples and the South. Outside of Italy, this region's cooking is sometimes all that the adventurous diner can find. Tomatoes, garlic, onions and herbs combine to lend their character to all dishes designated *alla* PIZZAIOLA. Naples itself is the birthplace of the pizza. From the coastal waters come the shellfish for clam soup (*zuppa di vongole*) or clam sauces for pasta. Eggplant is immensely popular; it is often layered and baked with Parmesan cheese, *alla Parmigiana.* Neapolitan sweetmakers create the celebrated *biscuit* TORTONI and the fruit ices called GRANITE.

Sicily. Stuck out in the Mediterranean at the toe of Italy's boot, this island has been influenced over the centuries by wave after wave of seafarers: Greeks, Arabs, Africans, Turks. All have left their mark on its cuisine. The masterpiece of the Sicilian kitchen is the eggplant stew called CAPONATA, which in its subtle combination of sweet and sour flavors, shows a Middle Eastern influence. That influence is even more evident in the island's pastries and cakes, particularly the CANNOLI, Turkish in origin, and the rich layer cake called CASSATA .

à l'ITALIENNE (FR)

In French, the phrase "Italian-style" has two distinct meanings: With any variety of PASTA it refers to the simplest Italian treatment for noodles—butter and Parmesan cheese. For the French preparation of meats, poultry, fish or vegetables, it refers to any dish garnished with an abundance of mushrooms.

Few of us are adventurous in the matter of food; in fact, most of us think there is something disgusting in a bill of fare to which we are unused.
—WILLIAM JAMES

JAMBALAYA (US)

The American South's answer to PAELLA. This Creole speciality contains rice, wine, broth, ham, sausage, chicken, shrimp, crab, tomatoes, okra, onions, peppers, chilies, garlic and just about anything else at hand. It has the consistency of a very thick soup, so it is best served in bowls.

JAPANESE COOKING

The islands' cooking is an art born of austerity. On those crowded, rocky islands, the people have learned over the centuries to take even the most meager offerings of the seasons and to prepare and present them with an exquisite yet simple beauty that pleases the eye and the soul as much as the appetite. The two predominant seasonings are the seaweed stock called DASHI and a light soy sauce; they combine with marvelous seafoods, sparing quantities of meats, beautiful fresh vegetables, rice and noodles to make a cuisine that bears out the artistic adage that "less

JAPANESE COOKING ─────────────

is more.'' A Japanese banquet will be composed
of small portions of many different kinds of
dishes, from the dozen or so main categories into
which the cuisine may be divided:

Aemono are composed salads of vegetables or
fish with a thick dressing based on tofu, MISO
paste or crushed sesame seeds.

Agemono covers all manner of batter- or
breadcrumb-coated deep-fried foods, the most
famous example being TEMPURA.

Gohanmono covers all rice dishes—plain boiled
rice; casseroles of rice, meat and vegetables; and
the popular luncheon meals consisting of a large
bowl of rice topped with morsels of food, *donburi*.

Menrui are noodles: thin ones made from buckwheat (*soba*); fine, white wheat noodles (*sōmen*);
broad wheat noodles (UDON); and others. They
may be cooked and served in broth, drained and
tossed with dried *nori* (seaweed shreds) and
WASABI (horseradish), or braised like a meatless
SUKIYAKI and so on.

Mushimono are steamed dishes, particularly of
vegetables, seafood or chicken. Usually a selection of ingredients is first arranged in its serving
dish and then cooked in the steamer. CHAWAN-
MUSHI is an excellent example of such a steamed
assembly.

Nabemono are one-pot meals, cooked and eaten
communally: meat, poultry or seafood, with vegetables, braised at table in a fragrant liquid. See
SHABU-SHABU and SUKIYAKI.

Nimono are simmered dishes—fillets of fish gently cooked in *sake* and soy sauce, for example, or
shrimp simmered with squash and spinach in
DASHI, *mirin* (sweet rice wine) and soy.

Sashimi is sliced raw fish. Molded with vinegared rice, it also becomes an important variety
of SUSHI. Both are often eaten as meals in themselves, and they are given separate entries in this
book.

Shirumono are soups. *Suimono,* or clear soups,
are epitomized by DASHI; so-called thick soups,
still relatively light and clear, include the common
MISO soup, with its cloud of soy bean paste. The

soups are sparingly garnished with finely cut pieces of vegetable, cubes of tofu and sometimes morsels of fish.

Sunomono are vinegared salads served as side dishes. They may be made from any raw or cooked vegetable, and some feature morsels of seafood such as octopus or crab.

Tsukemono are an endless assortment of beautiful pickles, cured in salt or vinegar with seasonings: fine slivers of ginger, tiny whole plums or apricots, coins of carrot, thick slices of DAIKON or shreds of cabbage with flakes of hot chili.

Yakimono means "grilled things" and covers any pan-fried, broiled or grilled food: seafoods, meats and vegetables. Whole grilled fish is a specialty, but generally the food is smaller or lighter—the cubes of chicken skewered for YAKI-TORI are a popular example.

à la JARDINIÈRE (FR)

Like an artful display of gardener's produce, this garnish surrounds roast meat or poultry with neat groupings of green beans, carrot and turnip balls, white kidney beans, peas and cauliflower florets with HOLLANDAISE.

JERKY (US)

The name conjures up images of cowboys chewing on these tough strips of air-dried salted beef. It is curious to note that the word and the food have become so accepted that the curing process for the beef is now actually known as "jerking." The word in fact derives from the old Spanish *charquit*, meaning "sliced and dried," and the cowboys who first enjoyed jerky were Mexican.

JUGGED (UK)

An adjective most often applied to a stew of hare but also used with other kinds of game, meat and poultry. It is prepared in a large, covered earthenware crock (in old parlance, a "jug"). The meat is often marinated for up to two days in vinegar or red wine before it is cooked. Other ingredients in the stew are brandy, lemon juice, onions, mushrooms, bacon and herbs. The blood of the hare, mixed with a little flour, is sometimes used to thicken the stew. It is eaten simply, with a crisp salad and noodles or bread.

JULIENNE (FR)

Describes any food cut into long, thin strips: the large pieces of meat, cheese and vegetable of a chef's salad; the fine shreds of aromatic vegetable that flavor and moisten a fish cooked *en* PAPILLOTE; the matchsticks of TRUFFLE that might decorate a lavish CHAUD-FROID. Clear broth garnished with fine strips of vegetable is known as consomeé *julienne*.

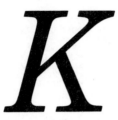

*In the affairs of the mouth,
the strictest punctuality is
indispensable—the gastronomer
ought to be as accurate an observer
to Time as the astronomer.*
                    —WILLIAM KITCHINER

KABABS (IN)

A catch-all word for small pieces of meat, broiled or fried and served as hors d'oeuvres or main courses. Some bear a close resemblance to the Middle Eastern KEBABS, but others seem related in name alone. Best loved are the following:

Boti kabab—pieces of lamb are marinated with yogurt and spices, skewered and charcoal-grilled.

Nargis kabab—a whole hardboiled egg is coated with a thick mixture of ground lamb, tomatoes, onions and spices, then dipped in egg white and deep-fried. *Nargis* means "narcissus," a white and yellow flower with a cup-shaped corona resembling the cut-open kabab. It tastes like a hot SCOTCH EGG.

Pasanda kabab—strips of the finest lamb fillet (*pasanda* means "fillet") are pounded thin, briefly marinated with spices and charcoal grilled on bamboo skewers.

Seek kabab—ground lamb is mixed with

cooked, dried yellow peas, lots of spices or herbs, then shaped into small patties and shallow-fried.

Tikka kabab—lamb, chicken or fish pieces are marinated with yogurt, ginger, spices and red food dye, then skewered and cooked in a TANDOORI oven.

KEBABS (ME)

These charcoal-grilled skewers of meat or poultry are popular as hors d'oeuvres or main courses throughout the eastern Mediterranean lands. Sometimes they consist simply of the meat itself—lamb, beef, pork or chicken. Often the meat is marinated with olive oil, lemon juice, garlic, herbs and spices for more flavor and to tenderize tough cuts. In more elaborate versions like the Turkish lamb or mutton shish kebab, the pieces of meat are alternated with whole mushrooms, cherry tomatoes and chunks of green pepper and onion. In this classic form, the kebab will most likely be served on a rice PILAF, perhaps dressed with a simple tomato sauce. But kebabs are just as likely to be served on their own or, for a handy lunch, slipped from their skewers into whole hot PITA bread with salad—a Middle Eastern sandwich. Relatives of the kebab are also served in the cuisines of the East: the Indians, for example, have all manner of KABABS, and the Indonesians have their bamboo-skewered SATAYS.

KEDGEREE (UK)

A marvelous part of the traditional English breakfast, it is a mixture of flaked smoked haddock, rice and curry spices topped with slices of hardboiled egg. As the seasoning suggests, the dish originated in colonial India as *khichari,* a lentil-and-rice mixture.

KEFTEDES (ME/GR)

Greek fried meatballs, made with ground beef or veal and breadcrumbs, bound by egg. The meatballs are distinctively aromatic, a result of the flavorings added to the mixture: onion, oregano, mint, parsley, vinegar and olive oil. They are served as a main course; smaller versions, known by the diminutive *keftedakia*, are a popular hors d'oeuvre, or *meze*. See also the Turkish KÖFTE.

KIBBEH (ME)

A Lebanese appetizer or main course. Kibbeh is made by pounding together raw lamb, burghul (cracked wheat), onion, fresh mint, olive oil and spices. The smooth, aromatic paste may be eaten raw as *kibbeh nayyeh*; shaped into balls or patties and then fried; or layered in a pan with a lamb and pine-nut mixture and then baked. Kibbeh may also be made from beef, chicken or fish, though these are not as common. Jordanians called the dish *kobbah;* Iraqis call it *kubbah*.

KIELBASA (EE)

The most famous Polish sausage, it is made from a mixture of chopped pork and pork fat liberally laced with garlic. The sausage is air-dried and served in thin slices as a cold cut, or it may be poached. It is an essential ingredient in the Polish national dish, BIGOS.

KIEV (RUS)

Although this style of cooking boned chicken breasts is today international restaurant fare, it originated in the Ukrainian capital. In its classic form it is made from skinless chicken breasts with the rib bones removed but the wing bone left attached, forming a cutlet shape. After the breast meat is pounded flat, a finger of frozen butter is placed in the middle of each breast, and the meat is folded

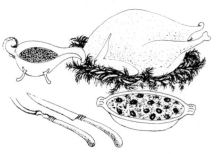

around it. Then the stuffed breasts are double-coated with egg and breadcrumbs and deep-fried. When a portion is cut open, the butter filling—now melted—spurts out to bathe the succulent meat and crisp coating.

KIMCHI (SEA)

A tart and tangy pickle served with almost every meal. It is made from a mixture of cabbage, cucumbers, onions, radishes, garlic, ginger, salted fish paste and chilies—all fermented in a salt-water brine. Deceptively fresh and cool in appearance, kimchi may be overpoweringly strong to the unwary.

KIPPER (UK)

Choice herrings are cleaned and split down the back, soaked briefly in brine and then smoked for about half a day to make kippers. A good kipper has plump, pale-brown flesh and a surprisingly delicate, not-too-fishy flavor—all perfect qualities for a breakfast fish. The old-fashioned way to prepare one for eating is to put it tail up in a heat-proof jug, add boiling water and let the kipper soak for ten minutes; alternatively, it may be broiled or pan-fried in butter. Kippers are excellent either alongside or flaked and mixed with scrambled eggs; they are also a key ingredient in KEDGEREE.

KISHKA (JE)

Means "intestines," but this dish is definitely not tripe. Like sausage, it uses the gut as a casing for a well-seasoned mixture of flour, mashed barley, onions, a little chicken SCHMALTZ and maybe some finely chopped carrot. Boiled, then baked, and served in slices, the kishka, also known more delicately as stuffed derma, is eaten as an appetizer or side dish, with or without its casing.

KNACKWURST

See WURSTS.

KÖFTE (ME)

Like the Greek KEFTEDES, these are made from ground meat—in this case mutton or lamb, mixed with breadcrumbs and seasoned with olive oil and onion. Unlike the Greek dish, köfte is shaped into patties and grilled on skewers over charcoal.

KÖNIGSBERGER KLOPS (GE)

The city of Königsberg was capital of East Prussia; its best-known dish remains these dumplinglike meatballs of beef, pork, breadcrumbs and egg, unusually flavored with anchovies, capers and onion. The klops are poached, then served with an equally sharp-flavored sauce, made of sour cream, lemon juice, capers, anchovies, cloves, allspice and bay. The dish was a favorite of the philosopher Immanuel Kant.

KOREAN COOKING

It tastes like a hybrid of the northern Chinese and the Japanese kitchens: a spicy cuisine, making lavish use of chilies and garlic, yet exhibiting a spare simplicity. The Korean *sinsullo* is a native version of the Chinese FIRE POT, while KIM CHEE, or pickled cabbage, resembles some varieties of Japanese TSUKEMONO.

KORMA or KURMA (IN)

A special Mogul variation on braised meat. The braising liquid, subtly spiced, is thick with cream, yogurt and ground almonds or cashews or puréed fruit. The finest meat is used—usually lamb fillet or chicken breasts—and it is marinated in the cooking liquid before braising. After cooking, the sauce is rich and velvety, clinging to the meat.

KRUPUK (SEA)

Indonesian deep-fried chips served as a snack or a garnish, made from a mixture of shrimp and manioc flour. Before cooking, they look like flat, brittle, milk-white flakes about the size of a poker chip; in hot oil they quickly puff up, at least tripling in size, and turn light and crisp. The Chinese make similar shrimp crackers, artificially colored in pastel shades, that have far less flavor than the true Indonesian product.

KUGEL (JE)

Its name is a Yiddish variation on the German word for the square-cornered shallow pan in which this hefty pudding of broad egg noodles or shredded potatoes is baked. Noodle (in Yiddish, *lokshen*) kugel is usually sweet, with cinnamon and raisins; potato kugel is savory, with onions and, perhaps, chicken SCHMALTZ. Kugel is a cornerstone of Jewish home cookery: in *The Joys of Yiddish,* Leo Rosten recalls the old Yiddish saying, "If a woman can't make a kugel—divorce her."

KUGELHOPF

See GUGELHUPF.

KULEBIAKA (RUS)

Flaky pastry encloses a rich filling based on salmon or cabbage in this elegant Russian luncheon or dinner main course. The kulebiaka is baked in a large loaf-form sliced at table and eaten garnished with sour cream.

KUNG PAO (CH)

Named for an esteemed member of the imperial court who was forced into exile, this style of stir-fried dish includes sliced beef or chicken, whole prawns or other pieces of seafood tossed with chili paste, bean sauce, chunks of dried red chili pepper and roasted peanuts. To the uninitiated, the chili pepper pieces can be unbelievably hot. Those without fire-proof palates should avoid eating them. A touch of fire remains in the sauce.

All civilized nations cook their food, to improve its taste and digestibility. The degree of civilization is often measured by the cuisine.
—MARY LINCOLN

LACHSSCHINKEN
See HAMS.
LAOS ROOT (SEA)
Relative of ginger. This dried seasoning appears in Indonesian braises.
LASAGNE
See PASTA.
LASAGNETTE
See PASTA.

LATIN AMERICAN COOKING
The cuisine of note in Latin America is that of Mexico (see MEXICAN COOKING). Otherwise, most of the nations in Central and South America lack cuisines of international ranking. Two Latin American nations stand above the others:
Brazilian cooking is renowned for the wonders wrought on native ingredients by the West African slaves who were transported to the country. The most noteworthy example of their influence is the Brazilian national dish, FEIJOADA, a highly seasoned meal of smoked and fresh meats cooked

with black beans and served with manioc meal and spicy garnishes.

Peru. Here Spanish cooking combined with that of the Incan Empire to produce two distinctive but related "creole" cuisines, one in the coastal lowlands, the other high in the Andes. The former is a light but chili-spiced cookery emphasizing seafood; CEVICHE, a beautiful dish of raw fish "cooked" by the acid in citrus juice, and garnished with such Incan staples as corn and sweet potatoes, exemplifies the cuisine. A great deal of cooking along the coast is done over charcoal, and vendors sell from street-corner braziers one of the country's most popular meat dishes, the skewered chunks of marinated beef heart called ANTICUCHOS. Mountain cooking is heartier and less sophisticated than that of the coast; its predominant ingredient is the Incan gift to the world, the potato, most often served with a sauce of cheese, milk and the local variety of chili pepper called *aji*.

LATKE (JE)

Potato pancakes prepared year-round but especially during the Hanukkah festival. They are made from grated raw potatoes, onion, eggs and seasonings; the mixture is sometimes extended with MATZO meal. Pan-fried until browned and crisp, they are usually presented as a course or a light meal in their own right, garnished with sour cream, apple sauce or preserves; they may also be served unadorned as a side dish.

LEBERWURST

See WURSTS.

à la LIMOUSINE (FR)

Named after the Limousin region in south-central France, it is, first, a style of cooking red cabbage, by braising it with broth, a little pork fat and chopped chestnuts. Any dish garnished with red cabbage may also be graced with the name; thus, the typical rib roast of pork in the Limousin is a *carré de porc à la limousine*.

LINGUE DI PASSERO

See PASTA.

LINGUINE

See PASTA.

LINZERTORTE (AU)

A speciality from the town of Linz, this tart appears in every Viennese pastry shop. It has as its base a dough of ground almonds, flour, lemon peel and spices. Pressed into a round or rectangular tart pan, it is filled with a shallow layer of raspberry jam. The tart's most distinctive feature comes next: Narrow strips of the almond dough are placed on top in a latticework pattern before baking.

LION'S HEAD (CH)

This specialty of Shanghai consists of large steamed meatballs made from finely ground pork, seasoned with soy, rice wine, scallions and ginger. Served on a bed of cabbage, the meatballs are said to resemble the heads of lions, the cabbage their manes.

alla LIVORNESE (IT)

The coastal province of Leghorn (Livorno) in Tuscany is famed for seafood and makes lavish use of tomatoes, onions, garlic, anchovies and olive oil. All these ingredients come together in many Livornese dishes, such as *tonno* (tuna) and *triglie* (red mullet) *alla livornese*. The province's most famous dish, *cacciucco alla livornese* is a kind of BOUILLA-BAISE with tomatoes, onions and garlic.

LONTONG (SEA)

White rice is boiled in closed cylindrical containers; after more than an hour, the rice grains, swollen and pressed together, form a solid rice cake—lontong. The cake may be eaten warm or cold, whole or sliced, plain or dipped in a spicy sauce. It plays the same role as bread, as a picnic or traveling food, or as a garnish for skewers of SATAY and other foods.

LOX (JE)

A type of smoked salmon. The word derives from the German *lachs* and the Scandinavian *lax,* as in GRAVLAX. But lox is never served alone, as smoked salmon would be. It appears, rather, in omelets, often combined with onions or—the truest Jewish way to eat it—with slathers of cream cheese on a plain or toasted bagel—topped with thin slices of red onion.

LUGANEGA (IT)

Northern Italian fresh sausage, made in long, thin casings from a mixture of coarsely chopped pork and cooked usually by grilling. The name is a salute to the region of Lucania, in Italy's boot, famed for the superiority of its preserved meats. That fame has spread beyond Italy: similar Mediterranean fresh sausages bear their own adaptations of the name, such as the Greek *loukanikah*; and so do some cured, salami-type sausages, like the Bulgarian *loukanka*.

à la LYONNAISE (FR)

Onions are the chief produce of the Lyonnais, in eastern central France, and plenty of sautéed onions—with perhaps a dash of vinegar and some parsley—garnish the dishes of this region. The name applies to dishes such as omelets with onion filling, pan-fried potatoes with onions, tripe-and-onion stew, and steaks and roasts with onions.

M

*The pleasant hours of our life are
all connected, by a more or less
intangible link, with some memory
of the table.*

—CHARLES MONSELET

MACCHERONI
See PASTA.

MACÉDOINE (FR) *or* **MACEDONIA** (IT)
Refers to mixtures of diced fresh fruits in
syrup. It is served as a dessert or with diced
cooked vegetables, presented hot or cold
with butter or a dressing as a side dish or
salad. The name refers fancifully to the country of Macedonia: a collection of tiny separate
states—analogous to little dice, perhaps—
that were consolidated into a nation by Alexander the Great.

à la MÂCONNAISE (FR)
The region of Mâcon, in Burgundy, produces
hearty red wines. Any food braised or
poached in the local red wine—even fish—will
bear the region's name.

MAFALDE
See PASTA.

MAÎTRE D'HÔTEL butter (FR)
A topping for steak or for grilled or deep-fried
fish. It is made by creaming together butter,

lemon juice, parsley, salt and pepper. It gets its name from the hotel master, the "maître d'," who supervises the dining room of a large restaurant.

MALOSSOL CAVIAR

See ROES.

MANHATTAN CLAM CHOWDER

See CHOWDER.

MANICHE

See PASTA.

MARCHAND DE VIN (FR)

Means "wine merchant" and describes a sauce usually served over steak. It is made from shallots, red wine and stock; reduced to a strong concentrate; and finished with butter, lemon juice and parsley.

à la MARÉCHALE (FR)

The "field marshall" style of cooking small cuts of chicken or veal involves coating them with egg and breadcrumbs and frying them in butter. A garnish of asparagus tips, and sometimes TRUFFLES, completes the dish.

MARENGO (FR)

Dunand, chef to Napoleon Bonaparte, invented this chicken dish impromptu on the battlefield after his master had defeated the Austrians at the Battle of Marengo. Using what was at hand, the chef took chicken pieces and sautéed them with oil, garlic, tomatoes and brandy (from the emperor's flask), garnishing the dish with steamed crayfish from a local stream and fried eggs. Napoleon, to whom it was served on a tin plate, told his chef, "Feed me like this after every battle." The crayfish—a culinary anomaly in chicken dishes—embarrassed Dunand, but his effort to substitute mushrooms for the offending crustaceans was rebuffed by Napoleon, who claimed the change might bring bad luck. Nowadays, crayfish and egg are sometimes left out; veal is also cooked Marengo style, never including those garnishes.

alla MARINARA (IT)

"Sailor's" style though this PASTA sauce may

be, it includes no seafood—just fresh tomatoes, garlic, olive oil and basil or oregano. The only nautical connection is its hometown, the seaport of Naples.

MARJOLAINE (FR)

It consists of four long, narrow spongecakes dense with ground almonds and hazelnuts, separated in turn by a bitter chocolate cream made with CRÈME FRAÎCHE, a buttercream made with CRÈME CHANTILLY and a second buttercream flavored with powdered almond PRALINE. The sides of the cake are covered with chocolate shavings, the top decorated with powdered sugar, and the cake—intensely rich—is served in narrow slices.

MARMITE

See PETITE MARMITE.

alla MARSALA (IT)

The sweet, fortified Sicilian wine Marsala gives its name to any dish—particularly breaded veal cutlets—dressed with a syrupy sauce made from the wine, broth and butter.

MATAMBRE (LA)

Means "kill hunger," a promise more than fulfilled by this Argentine appetizer. A thin sheet of flank steak is covered with spinach, whole carrots and hardboiled eggs, onions, peppers, garlic, bacon and anything else that might strike the cook's fancy. It is then rolled up tightly, tied, poached and left to cool. Served in crosswise slices that reveal a spiraling mosaic, the matambre is eaten with a *salsa* of fresh parsley, garlic, oil and vinegar.

MATELOTE (FR)

The name for a sailor's wife and, by extension, for the mixed fish stew she makes with wine, onions and mushrooms.

MATJES

See HERRINGS.

MATSUTAKE

See MUSHROOMS.

MÉCHOUI (ME)

This dish is to Algerian cuisine what roast beef is to British. In the traditional fashion of the nomads who originated the dish, a whole lamb is spitted and roasted for hours over hot embers, basted continuously, until it is so tender that the meat can be picked from the bones by hand. In the city, méchoui is more likely to be cooked on a conventional barbecue, with smaller cuts of meat.

MEE KROB (SEA)

The most delightful Thai noodle dish. Thin, transparent rice noodles are broken into small pieces; deep-fried, they puff up light and crisp. The noodles are tossed with a sweet-and-sour sauce containing bits of pork, shrimp, crabmeat, onions and garlic. Heaped in a mound on a serving dish, they are garnished with fresh coriander leaves, bean sprouts and chopped peanuts.

MENRUI

See JAPANESE COOKING.

METTWURST

See WURSTS.

MEUNIÈRE (FR)

A style of cooking fish, particularly sole. The fillets, dusted with seasoned flour (which explains the name—*meunière* means "miller's wife"), are gently browned in butter, then dressed in their serving plate with lemon juice, chopped parsley and melted butter.

MEXICAN COOKING.

Mexico's cuisine clearly shows its Aztec roots, particularly in its use of corn. That staple, dried and ground, is the basis of the TAMAL and, more significantly, the TORTILLA—Mexico's versatile daily bread, which is eaten as it comes from the griddle or transformed into TACOS, ENCHILADAS, CHILAQUILES, CHALUPAS, FLAUTAS or crisp chips for scooping up GUACAMOLE. Chilies and chocolate were two other Aztec delicacies. Both are still popular today: dozens of different kinds of chilies flavor Mexican dishes; hot chocolate, flavored with cinnamon and beaten until frothy, is a popular breakfast drink. Both chocolate and chili are key elements of MOLE, an ancient Aztec sauce in which turkey is simmered to make the country's national dish, *mole poblano de guajalote*. Chicken is a frequent substitute. Another strong Mexican influence can be traced to the Mayan culture in the Yucatán, where spicy, steamed dishes called PIBIL are still prepared following ancient formulas. The Spanish conquest of Mexico brought more sophistication to the country's kitchen, but in fact, Mexico had a greater impact on Spain's cooking: conquistadores carried such New World ingredients as tomatoes, peppers and chocolate back to Europe.

MIDDLE EASTERN COOKING

Robustly Mediterranean, the cuisine is full of sun-ripened vegetables, of pungent and aromatic herbs, of meats and fish cooked over charcoal in the open air. Eggplant, peppers and tomatoes abound. Oregano sharpens flavors, mint sweetens them; garlic and onions lend bite. Olive oil (see OILS) bathes salads, meats and vegetables alike, its suaveness matched by the crushed sesame-seed paste, TAHINI. Bread is coarse and crusty, baked in loaves or in flat, oval pockets called PITA. Few Middle Eastern specialties are confined to a single country: the nomadic lives of Arabs and the glorious days of the Ottoman Empire have both spread far and wide what once were local dishes. Some highlights of the major cuisines:

Greece. Although Greeks are loath to admit it, some of their most famous dishes are remnants of Ottoman rule: DOIMATHES, MOUSSAKA and BAKLAVA are all Turkish in origin, all still enjoyed in that country too. Other, more original dishes include the egg-and-lemon soup or sauce called AVGOLE-MONO; the macaroni-and-lamb casserole called PASTITSO; SPANAKOPITTA with its filling of spinach and the country's marvelous feta cheese; and the creamy dip of smoked ROE, TARAMASALATA, one of the mainstays of the Greek hors d'oeuvre spread known as *meze* (a custom found in various forms, and variously spelled, throughout the region). Another popular *meze* dish, HUMMUS, is actually

Arabic in origin, but the Greeks love it.

Lebanon. Its cuisine emphasizes seafood, but lamb is also popular; cinnamon, cayenne and paprika create a flavor at once sweet and fiery. The Lebanese are also responsible for the two finest dishes involving the widespread Middle Eastern grain called burghul, the mint-scented salad called TABBOULEH and the raw or cooked paste of lamb and burghul known as KIBBEH.

Turkey. Its specialties epitomize the Middle Eastern cuisine. Aside from those already mentioned under Greece, there are turnovers of PHYLLO dough, BÖREK, and the various KEBABS.

MILLE-FEUILLE (FR)

Literally it means "a thousand leaves," which may be an exaggeration, but this puff-pastry assembly certainly gives that impression. Layers of the baked flaky puff pastry are stacked several inches high, alternating with a thick pastry cream custard or some other rich, creamy filling such as CRÈME CHANTILLY; the top is dusted with confectioner's sugar. A dark-roasted coffee, *au lait* or espresso, goes perfectly with the pastry.

MINCEUR

See FRENCH COOKING.

MIROTON (FR)

This is what wise French housewives (and restaurateurs) do with their leftover beef. They slice it into small, thin pieces and put it in a casserole with a sauce of onions, stock, vinegar and herbs. On top, they sprinkle buttered breadcrumbs, and then they bake the dish until the crumbs turn golden. Garnished with chopped parsley, the beef makes a headily aromatic main course for lunch or dinner.

MISO (JA)

A thick, sour, slightly salty paste of fermented soybeans and rice, it is a widely used seasoning and soup base. There are two basic kinds—white *shiru* (actually a tan color) and black or red *aka* (reddish brown), depending on the variety of soybean and the proportion of rice; the darker the paste, the stronger it is, but the two kinds are interchangeable in use. Dissolved in boiling water, miso is a staple breakfast drink; with piles of vegetable, seaweed and tofu added, it is the preeminent Japanese soup. Vegetables, meat or fish pickled with miso are called *misozuke; nasu no misoni,* eggplant sautéed with miso and DASHI, is a favorite side dish or appetizer.

à la MODE (FR/US)

"In the fashion" is the literal translation, but it means "in the popular style" and refers to two distinctly different preparations. In France, it is a beef dish, *boeuf à la mode:* A large cut of meat is poached in broth and wine with calfs' feet, carrots, onions, celery and turnips, then served with the vegetables, moistened with the cooking liquid. The calfs' feet give the liquid a gelatinous quality, and the beef may also be molded in the resulting ASPIC and served cold. In the United States, à la mode is the popular way to serve pie: with a scoop of ice cream.

à la MOELLE (FR)

The word means "bone marrow." The rich garnish for grilled steaks, contains marrow prepared in a sauce of veal stock, wine, shallots, butter and herbs.

MOLE (MEX)

From the Aztec *molli,* referring to any sauce made with hot or sweet chili, the name now refers to a very specific type of sauce: a concoction of chilies, onions, garlic, tomatoes, raisins, almonds and spices, thickened with TORTILLAS and—its most renowned feature—enriched with unsweetened chocolate, which makes it incomparably suave. Mole, pronounced MOH-LAY, may sauce any meat or poultry, but when turkey is simmered in it, the result is Mexico's national dish—*mole poblano de guajalote.* The *guajalote* is the bird. *Poblano* refers to the town of Puebla, where, legend has it, the dish was invented. Nuns at the convent of Santa Rosa, so the story goes, were suddenly faced with the imminent arrival of a viceroy and an archbishop, only to discover that they had nothing special enough to serve to such distinguished guests. The mole's unlikely combination of ingredients is supposedly the fortuitous result of their desperation: They killed a scrawny turkey, added everything else they could find and prayed. The result was culinary heaven.

MONGOLIAN FIRE POT (CH)
See FIRE POT.

MONK'S VEGETABLES (CH)
Buddhist monks are strictly vegetarian, and this dish ensures they get a well-balanced diet. Bamboo shoots, snow peas, bean sprouts, Chinese cabbage, spinach, broccoli, whole baby sweet corn, cloud ear fungus and Chinese mushrooms (see MUSHROOMS) are stir-fried with protein-rich TOFU. The dish is also known as Buddha's Delight.

à la MONTMORENCY (FR)
Named after a Paris suburb and the excellent cherries grown there, the name applies to any dish made with cherries.

MONTPELLIER (FR)
Describes an intensely green butter colored with a mixture of chopped FINES HERBES and spinach. The flavor is boosted further with gherkins, capers, anchovies and garlic; olive oil and raw egg yolk add further richness. Whisked to a light smoothness, the butter traditionally garnishes cold fish plates.

MOO SHU PORK (CH)
This popular Northern specialty began as a peasant dish that made economical use of leftovers. Shredded pork is tossed over heat with scallions, clour ear fungus (see MUSHROOMS); tiger-lily buds (long, golden buds from the tree, chewy and slightly acidic); raw egg; soy sauce; and rice wine. The soft, moist mixture is enfolded in crêpelike wheat pancakes and eaten by hand.

MOREL

See MUSHROOMS.

MORNAY sauce (FR)

A dressing for fish, chicken, eggs or vegetables, it consists of a BÉCHAMEL combined with grated Gruyère or Parmesan cheese and, depending on the food it accompanies, fish stock, chicken stock, or cream. If the dish is cooked as a GRATIN, the Mornay sauce gives it a beautiful brown coating.

MORTADELLA (IT)

"The noblest of all pork products" is how this large, cured sausage, a specialty of Bologna, was identified by one seventeenth-century gourmet. Very finely minced pork is mixed with a mild blend of spices and tightly packed into casings, then air-dried. The sausage's exceptionally smooth texture is best appreciated in thin slices. The medieval monks who first prepared mortadella mashed the meat in a *mortaio della carne di maiale* (mortar for pork); eventually, they shortened and joined the first two words to give the sausage its name.

MOUSSAKA (GR) *or* **MUSSAKKA** (ME)

A casserole of layers of eggplant and a fragrant lamb and tomato sauce. It is often topped with a cheese soufflé mixture that gives it a puffy, golden surface. Moussaka is probably Arabic in origin and was introduced to Greece in the Middle Ages.

MOUSSELINE (FR)

Its various meanings are all connected with whipped cream. (The word *mousse* means "froth" in common usage.) When whipped cream is added to a sauce, the sauce takes on the word as an adjective: thus, HOLLANDAISE mousseline. Puréed raw fish, whisked together with cream over ice to form a light, firm paste, is shaped into balls and poached or pressed into a mold and baked to make fish mousselines—smooth, subtly flavored hors d'oeuvres served hot or cold, plain or sauced.

alla MUGNAIA (IT)

It is to fillets of *sogliole* what *à la* MEUNIÈRE is to fillets of sole.

MULLIGATAWNY (UK/IN)

A soup probably first made to suit the taste of English *sahibs* in colonial India. The name comes from the Tamil word *milakutanni,* which means "pepper water," but today's version is not very peppery. The piquancy of spices like coriander and red pepper is balanced by the velvety consistency of yogurt, coconut milk and sweet cream or even almond milk or peanut butter. Chicken broth and onions form the usual base, often with apples added. Lamb, beef or vegetable broth may be substituted.

MUSHIMONO

See JAPANESE COOKING.

MUSHROOMS

For the lover of good food accustomed to eating only the widely cultivated field mushroom (*Agaricus campestris*), there is a realm of wonderful mushrooms yet to be discovered—mushrooms of many shapes, sizes and color, with flavors even more beguiling than that of the familiar supermarket variety. Good restaurants, particularly French ones, will offer the best of the season's wild mushrooms; the Chinese and Japanese kitchens make imaginative use of their own distinctive varieties. Do take great caution when seeking mushrooms in the wild: while there are hundreds of edible species, so too are there many poisonous ones. Only an experienced mushroom hunter can tell for sure what to pick for eating.

Boletus (*Boletus edulis*). In France, this is known as the *cèpe;* in Italy, as *porcine.* With its domed, tan or brown cap, covered on the underside by tiny, fleshy tubes, this mushroom appears in the spring and autumn. Boleti have a rich, meaty flavor, excellent when they are sautéed in oil or butter and tossed with a PERSILLADE. Dried boleti flavor the gravies of rich stews such as the French DAUBE.

Chanterelle (*Cantherellus cibarius*). This golden, fluted trumpet, its bell 2 to 4 inches across, delights diners with its delicate flavor and wonderfully fleshy texture. Chanterelles are best when sautéed in butter, perhaps with a hint of garlic or shallots.

Chinese Mushroom or **Matsutake** (*Armilleria edodes*). A specialty of the Chinese and Japanese kitchens, this autumn species is sometimes known in English as a pine mushroom for the distinctive fragrance it has of the trees near which it grows. It is dark brown, thick-stemmed and meaty, enjoyed cut into thick slices and lightly grilled or mixed into stir-fried vegetables.

Cloud Ear or **Tree Ear.** Reconstituted in water, these dried black fungi become incredibly delicate, crinkly, floppy morsels—light as clouds, one supposes, and shaped like tiny ears. They are prized in Chinese cookery not so much for flavor as for their slippery yet slightly crunchy texture, stir-fried with meat or vegetables and added to soups—particularly HOT AND SOUR SOUP.

Enokitake. These most delicate, pale-yellow, slightly crisp mushrooms, no bigger than matchsticks, are eaten fresh in Japanese salads, lightly cooked in soups or *nabemono* (see JAPANESE COOKING) or grilled with fish or poultry. Their name comes from the tree stumps they grow on—those of the *enoki,* or Chinese hackberry.

Morel (*Morchella esculenta*). Some say this springtime mushroom is the finest of all to eat: it is hollow, with a beige-to-black honeycombed head atop a short, slender stalk. Morels are dried after picking; briefly soaked in water, they lend exquisite flavor to omelets or cream sauces.

Shiitake. The most widely used Oriental mushroom, this is commercially grown by injecting its spores into cut logs of the oaklike *shii* tree (*Pasania cuspidata*). Its dark-brown, velvety, circular caps are dried—whole, sliced or chopped—for indefinite storage; reconstituted in water for several hours, they lend a light, woodsy flavor to soups, stews and dishes of rice or noodles.

Routine in cuisine is a crime.
—EDOUARD NIGNON

NAAN (IN)

The best-known TANDOORI-cooked bread, it is made from a dough of flour, eggs, ghee (clarified butter), sugar, salt, milk and curds. Left for a few hours, the curds ferment, making the dough rise and giving it a characteristic sour flavor. The dough is divided and flattened into ovals just under one foot long, which are stuck by one end to the inside top wall of a hot tandoori oven. The naans bake in a matter of minutes, turning light brown, puffing slightly around the edges and stretching into a characteristic teardrop shape.

NABEMONO

See JAPANESE COOKING.

à la NAGE (FR)

Translates as "in the swim." It refers to a method of cooking crayfish, rock lobster or tiny lobsters, in *court bouillon,* a light poaching liquid of water, white wine and aromatic vegetables. The crustaceans are served "swimming" in that liquid, hot or cold.

à la NANTUA (FR)

Nantua is a town in eastern France known for its crayfish, so a fish dish garnished with these sweet freshwater crustaceans bears the town's name. So does a sauce for seafood, made of butter and puréed crayfish with cream, egg yolks and a pinch of cayenne pepper.

NAVARIN (FR)

A stew of lamb or mutton. Chunks of the meat are browned in oil, sprinkled with sugar that caramelizes to produce a rich brown sauce, dusted with flour as a thickener and simmered in white wine with vegetables. The vegetables may be nothing more than cubes of potato, but when carrots, onions, new potatoes and fresh green peas are included, the stew is known as a navarin *printanier*—a "springtime" lamb stew.

à la NEIGE (FR)

It means "in the snow," an apt description for eggs (*oeufs*) prepared as one of the classic desserts. The yolks go into a rich vanilla custard, which is poured onto a shallow serving dish. The whites are beaten with sugar and poached to make meringues light as snow drifts, which float atop the custard. Therein lies the dessert's English name, "floating islands."

NEWBURG (US)

An elegant style of preparing lobster, created at the celebrated Delmonico's in New York. The raw lobster is shelled; its meat is cut into chunks that are sautéed in butter and finished with a cream-and-sherry sauce thickened with egg yolks and seasoned with paprika.

NEW ENGLAND CLAM CHOWDER

See CHOWDER.

NIÇOISE (FR)

Nice, in Provence, is the major city of Mediterranean France, and its style of cooking embraces that region's key ingredients: tomatoes, garlic, olives, olive oil and anchovies. All these may find their way into the local seafood stews and sautées. And in the famed *salade Niçoise,* they join lettuce, tuna, string beans, green peppers, radishes and capers. Whether casually tossed in a bowl or beautifully arranged on a plate, the salad will be dressed with a VINAIGRETTE.

NIMONO

See JAPANESE COOKING.

NOCKERLN (AU)

The charmingly Germanic name for these little boiled egg-dough dumplings is actually of foreign origin: it's an adaptation of the Italian GNOCCHI. Tossed in melted butter, they are an especially good side dish with stews.

NORI

See SUSHI.

à la NORMANDE (FR)

Normandy is rich in apples and in cattle, and the Normans eat large quantities of both. The food of the region is heavy and smooth, typified by the famous *graisse normande,* a cooking fat made from beef kidneys, pork, vegetable essences and spices! When applied to veal or chicken, the designation à la Normande inevitably means with cream, apples and cider or Calvados (apple brandy). Calvados is so popular in the region that it is colloquially known as *le trou normand,* or "the Norman hole," perhaps referring to the throats with which it is so often in contact. The region also boasts a wealth of seafood; when fish is cooked in the local style, it will have an egg-enriched cream sauce and may be garnished with shrimp, oysters or mussels; a MATELOTE *à la Normande,* however, will be a mixed seafood stew with a sauce of cider, Calvados or cream.

NOUGAT (FR)

A stiff, chewy confection of honey, sugar syrup and beaten egg whites, packed with roasted almonds or hazelnuts and compressed under weights to ensure a dense consistency. The sweet is common throughout Europe, though it varies in the flavorings added and the kind of nuts used. In Italy, where it is called *torrone*, cocoa powder or melted chocolate is a frequent addition. Spaniards call the candy *turrón*.

NOUVELLE CUISINE
See FRENCH COOKING.

NOVA (JE)
The word is short for Nova Scotia, a source of smoked salmon. With typical Jewish linguistic ingenuity, the word has become an alternative to the Yiddish LOX; but Nova or lox, it's the same thing, eaten the same way. See also LOX.

NUOC MAM (SEA)
The basic seasoning in the Vietnamese kitchen, this factory-made sauce is prepared by layering fresh anchovies and salt in large barrels and leaving them to ferment for half a year. The finest nuoc mam, labeled *nhi*, is the first batch drained from the barrels. Interestingly, this sauce is quite similar to *garum*, the favorite fish sauce of the Roman empire.

NURNBERGERWURST
See WURSTS.

My heart shrank as I saw the restaurant Brébant *closed and dark...the ovens had only just been extinguished, the kitchens were still fragrant with vapors that exhaled the most exquisite savors....*
—ACHILLE OZANNE

OISEAUX SANS TÊTES (BNL/FR)

"Headless birds" is the fanciful name for rolled, stuffed slices of veal or beef. The meat is pounded thin and a stuffing of ham, bacon or sausage is placed on top. Rolled and tied with string, the little "birds" are browned in stock with onions, floured and braised in stock or beer. See also PAUPIETTES.

OLLA PODRIDA (IB)

"A grand dish," Don Quixote called it in Cervantes's epic novel, "eaten only by canons and bishops." Yet the name of this CO-CIDO on a heroic scale—a stew replete with game birds, sausages, cured and fresh pork and beef, pigs' ears and tails, chicken and abundant vegetables—translates as "putrid pot." The reason lies in the stew's catch-all character: in olden days, the round earthenware *olla* was never empty, always receiving new chunks of meat, more liquid, fresh vegetables. Ever on the simmer, it never really became putrid, but its contents developed a distinctive character that inspired affectionate derision.

ORECCHIETTE

See PASTA.

à l'ORIENTALE (FR)

The only thing even remotely oriental about this way of sautéing or braising fish, eggs or vegetables is the use of the exotic spice saffron. Otherwise, tomatoes and garlic complete the list of ingredients.

à l'ORLY (FR)

Fillets of fish, particularly whiting, prepared in this way are lightly battered, deep-fried and served with a fresh tomato sauce.

OSETROVA CAVIAR

See ROES.

OSSO BUCO (IT)

The name means "hollow bone." A Milanese braise, osso buco is made from meaty crosswise slices of veal shank, each with a bone full of marrow at its center. Cooked with wine, tomatoes, onions, garlic, carrots, celery and herbs and topped with an aromatic GREMO-LATA before serving, osso buco is accompanied by RISOTTO. After each diner has finished his meat, he spoons or sucks the delicate marrow from the bones.

P

The same intelligence is required to marshal an army in battle as to order a good dinner. The first must be as formidable as possible, the second as pleasant as possible, to the participants.

—PLUTARCH

PAELLA (IB)

A one-pot feast based on saffron rice, from the Levant on Spain's Mediterranean coast. It is replete with such diverse ingredients as clams and mussels; shrimp, crab and lobster; chicken and rabbit; fresh beef and pork; cured ham and smoked CHORIZO sausage; and tiny peas, green beans, chopped tomato, peppers, onions and garlic. Every town and every lover of paella has a favorite formula. The paella is simmered with olive oil (see OILS) and water in the wide, shallow, black iron pan—the *paellera*—that gives the dish its name.

PAGLIA E FIENO (IT)

"Straw and hay" is the image evoked by this mixture of yellow egg pasta and green spinach pasta. The dish can be sauced in many different ways, but the most popular is cream with peas and prosciutto (see HAMS).

PALACSINTEN (EE) *or* **PALATSCHINKEN** (AU)

Eastern European CRÊPES. These thin, round

egg-and-flour pancakes are rolled around a variety of fillings: fresh or preserved fruit, jam, melted chocolate, sweetened cheese or a chopped mixture of nuts, raisins and cream. Occasionally they are also served with savory fillings. They share a common origin with the Russian BLINI and the Jewish BLINTZ.

PANADE (FR)

A provincial soup of bread and hot water—but hardly subsistence fare when a sourdough country loaf is used and a final enrichment of egg yolks and butter is incorporated. The panade has limitless elaborations made by adding some sautéed leeks or garlic or onions or puréed squash; scraps of meat or poultry or sausage; good broth or milk or cream or wine. Made very thick, with less liquid, a simple panade is often used to bind stuffings for meat or fish.

PANETTONE (IT)

Milan's Christmas specialty, it is an exceptionally light yeast-leavened butter-and-egg pastry (much like the French BRIOCHE), studded with candied fruits. Its manufacture is big business in Milan, and excellent factory panettoni, wrapped airtight for freshness, are exported worldwide. Slices of the bread are delicious with dark-roasted espresso or cappuccino or a glass of brandy or Marsala.

PAPADUM (IN)

Light, crisp wafers made from lentil flour, served as a snack or an accompaniment to a curry. Before cooking, they are flat and brittle; dipped in hot oil, they puff up and expand in seconds. Most papadum are plain tasting, a nice contrast to fiery sauces. In northern Indian kitchens, chilies, pepper and other strong spices are mixed with the flour to contrast with the blander northern food. All papadum are delightful when dipped into CHUTNEYS or RAITAS.

en PAPILLOTE (FR)

Literally means ''in a bon-bon.'' Foods cooked in this way are sealed, seasoned and

117

baked in a half-moon-shaped packet of heavy-duty cooking paper. The bag puffs up with the steam built up during cooking, which is released once the diner opens the bag at table, revealing the fragrant, succulent food. Light meats such as poultry or veal are good cooked in this style, but fish en papillote is truly ·superb.

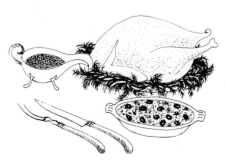

PAPPARDELLE
See PASTA.

PAPRIKÁS (EE)
A relative of GULYÁS. It is a paprika-flavored stew usually made with large chunks of chicken or veal. Unlike *gulyás,* it always includes sour or fresh cream, which gives it a rich, thick gravy.

PARATHA (IN)
The flakiest of the subcontinent's breads. It is made with an unleavened whole-wheat dough. Small balls of the dough are rolled out into thin circles about 5 inches across; brushed with *ghee* (clarified butter) or vegetable oil; then folded in half, brushed and folded again; then rolled out once more to make a triangle about 7 inches across. The paratha is cooked with butter or oil on a hot griddle developing a slightly crisp surface and a rich, nutty flavor. Still soft and pliant, the bread can be torn and dipped into the sauce of curries. It is also popular at breakfast in northern India, served with spicy scrambled

eggs. Puréed vegetables—especially potato, cauliflower or spinach—and spices are often stuffed inside the paratha before cooking, or even blended into the dough.

à la PARISIENNE (FR)

Cooked "in the style of Paris," potatoes are scooped into small balls, gently sautéed in butter, and then tossed and coated with a veal stock that has been boiled down to a thick syrup. Any meat or poultry dish garnished with these potatoes is also called à la Parisienne.

PARMA HAM

See HAMS.

PARMENTIER (FR)

Synonymous with potatoes. They can be puréed in soups, sliced and sautéed as a garnish for fried meats or poultry or mashed and used as a topping for a chopped-beef casserole (*haché Parmentier*). The term is a fitting tribute to the agronomist and economist Antoine-Auguste Parmentier, who in the late eighteenth and early nineteenth centuries campaigned for the use of the then widely disdained vegetable.

PASKHA (RUS)

Easter is the time for serving this traditional cheesecake molded in a four-sided pyramidal container. A sweetened blend of pot cheese, eggs, fresh or sour cream, almonds and candied fruits, the cake, once unmolded, is decorated with more candied fruits and served with the Russian yeast cake, *kulitsch*.

PASTA (IT)

Contrary to legend, Marco Polo did not discover pasta in China and carry it back to his home country at the end of the thirteenth century. Written records show Italians were eating pasta long before Marco Polo ever left for the East, and machines that look as though they might have been used to shape pasta were found in the ruins of Pompeii. Most pasta is made from a paste (hence the name) composed of hard durum wheat and water; eggs are sometimes added, and the pasta is sometimes colored green with puréed spinach. Over the centuries, the Italians have devised scores of shapes for pastas that may be boiled, baked or even deep-fried. Here are the most notable varieties:

Agnolotti—round ravioli: small pasta stuffed with chopped meat or ricotta and spinach.

Amorini—tiny cupid shapes for soup.

Anellini—tiny circles served in soup.

Anolini—small semicircular ravioli.

Bavette—like spaghetti, only oval in section.

Bucatini—"pierced" noodles, like macaroni.

Canneloni—very large tubes: boiled; stuffed with meat, spinach, ricotta and eggs; then baked.

Canolicchi—short, ribbed tubes.

Cappaletti—hat shapes, stuffed like ravioli.

Conchiglie—"conch shells," in shape.

Farfale—"butterflies," in shape.

Fettucelle—narrow fettucine.

Fettucine—"ribbons," often all' ALFREDO.

Fusilli—"spindles," thin squiggly noodles.

Gemelli—"twins," two short, entwined strands of spaghetti.

Gramigna—small tubes with a ribbed surface.

Lasagne—broad, long, flat egg or spinach noodles, layered and baked with cheese, meat, tomato sauce and BÉCHAMEL.

Lasagnette—like lasagne, only with wavy edges.

Lingue di pàssero—"sparrows' tongues," very narrow ribbons.

Linguine—"small tongues," thin, flat noodles.

Maccheroni—known in English as macaroni, short tubes.

Mafalde—long ribbons with fluted edges.

Maniche—short tubes.

Manicotti—"muffs," large tubes similar in shape and use to canneloni.

Mostaccioli—"little moustaches," in shape.

Orrecchiette—"little ears," small indented rounds.

Pappardelle—broad, short ribbons.

Penne—"pens," thin maccheroni with their

ends cut at a slant like quills.

Perciatelli—long, thin tubes.

Pulcini—chick-shaped tiny pasta for soup.

Ravioli—small squares stuffed with spinach and/or ricotta.

Rigatoni—large grooved tubes.

Ruote—''wagon wheels,'' in shape.

Tagliarini—small, thin tagliatelli.

Tagliatelli—egg ribbons somewhat wider than fettucine.

Tortellini—small, stuffed pasta shaped like ears. The Italians sometimes call them ''navels of Venus.''

Tortiglione—short, spiral twists like corkscrews.

Trenete—flattened spaghetti.

Vermicelli—''little worms,'' a thin variety of spaghetti.

Ziti—large macaronilike tubes.

PASTITSO (GR)

Macaroni and ground beef or lamb are the featured elements of this favorite family-style casserole. The meat—often left over from a roast—is simmered with tomatoes, onions, wine, oregano and, for a sweet edge, cinnamon; this mixture is layered with the cooked noodles. Like MOUSSAKA, the casserole is topped with a mixture of eggs, BÉCHAMEL and grated cheese; during baking, this puffs up like a soufflé, crowning the dish.

PASTY or CORNISH PASTY (UK)

Miners' wives in Cornwall make a sturdy pastry of flour, water and fat, using it to enclose meat, potatoes and other vegetables in hefty, half-moon turnovers that fit easily into their husbands' pockets. The home-cooked pasty is an economical repository for any and all leftovers; according to Cornish lore, the devil would not visit there, ''for fear of being baked in a pasty.'' Nowadays, hot or cold pasties with freshly cooked beef and vegetables make wonderful pub lunches with a pint of beer.

PÂTÉ (FR)

What to other nations is mere meatloaf, the French make into a culinary tour de force. A pâté is a mixture of chopped meats and seasonings, baked and served cold, in slices, as an hors d'oeuvre or a simple luncheon course with bread or toast. Pâtés vary enormously. Featured ingredients may be as refined as FOIE GRAS and TRUFFLES, as humble as pork. Seasonings and flavorings may be simply garlic, onions and fresh or dried herbs; but some pâtés are scented with liqueurs such as Grand Marnier or kirsch. A pâté's texture may be smooth and silky (a consistency befitting fine *foie gras*); or coarse and chewy, like the typical French *pâté de campagne,* or country pâté. Appropriate condiments may be elegantly chopped ASPIC or sharp-flavored CORNICHONS and mustard. A true pâté is encased in a pastry crust before baking (hence the name, from *pâte,* meaning "pastry"). But the term nowadays extends to what technically are known as *terrines,* those mixtures packed into earthenware baking dishes (*terrines*) before cooking. The name pâté also sometimes embraces GALLANTINES, boned poultry stuffed with pâtélike mixtures.

PAUPIETTES (FR)

Called "little corks," these stuffed rolls of beef or veal, wrapped in bacon and then browned and braised in stock, may indeed be cork-shaped. At a length of about 4 or 5 inches and a diameter of 2 inches or so, however, they are hardly little. The stuffing is some variety of chopped meat, mixed with vegetables or breadcrumbs and seasonings.

PAYASNAYA CAVIAR

See ROES.

à la PAYSANNE (FR)

Meat or poultry cooked "peasant style" is braised in stock and served with a rustic garnish of coarsely chopped carrots, turnips, onion and celery, all gently cooked in butter, along with fried pieces of bacon and little potatoes.

PEKING DUCK (CH)

The most famous dish of the capital's regal cuisine, it is a main course at once spectacular and informal. Plump, force-fed ducks (a breed from which the renowned Long Island duck was bred) are prepared first by separating (but not removing) the skin from the flesh; the skin is closed up tightly and the duck is roasted in a hot clay-oven and basted with honey and vinegar. The result: exceptionally crisp brown skin and succulent meat that is divided into small pieces by the waiter at table. Also presented are scallions with their ends sliced into brushlike tufts; small cucumber spears; thick, sweet-savory HOISIN sauce; and thin, crêpelike wheat pancakes about 4 inches across. With a scallion brush, each diner paints a pancake with HOISIN, then lays a piece of cucumber beside the scallion on the pancake; pieces of meat and skin are added, and the pancake is folded over the filling, rolled up and eaten by hand.

PENNE

See PASTA.

PEPERONATA (IT)

This cold, cooked vegetable hors d'oeuvre is a relative of the Sicilian CAPONATA and the French RATATOUILLE. It is made from sweet red and green peppers, onions and tomatoes and stewed in olive oil with garlic and herbs.

PERCIATELLI

See PASTA.

à la PÉRIGOURDINE (FR)

Périgord is the region of black TRUFFLES and FOIE GRAS. Any dish cooked or garnished with truffles will bear the region's name; in some cases, *foie gras* will also be included.

PERSILLADE (FR)

Made from chopped garlic and fresh parsley (*persil* in French) and added to braises and sautés at the end of cooking to give them a final bold burst of flavor. Leftover beef tossed in fat or oil and finished just with a persillade is known in French provincial cooking as a *persillade de boeuf.*

PESTO (IT)

The great basil sauce from the northwestern coastal city of Genoa. The bright and pungent herb is pounded with pine nuts (or walnuts), garlic, sharp Pecorino cheese and olive oil, creating a blend at once subtle and vibrant in flavor. Voluptuously thick, the sauce is served at room temperature over cooked ribbon pasta (trennette) or potato GNOCCHI. It may also be used as a salad dressing, particularly for sliced tomatoes. The sauce is also used as a table condiment to be stirred into individual bowls of minestrone soup, becoming *minestrone alla Genovese;* the same soup served across the French border in Provence is a *soupe au pistou.*

PETITE MARMITE (FR)

A *marmite* is an earthenware casserole; with the word *petite* affixed, it refers to a generous broth cooked in and served from an earthenware vessel. A country-style soup popularized in Parisian restaurants at the turn of the century, it includes beef, oxtail, chicken, marrow bones, onions, carrots, turnips, leeks, celery and cabbage simmered together in a light broth. The marrow is removed from the soup before serving and spread on toast to accompany the soup.

PETITS FOURS (FR)

"Little things from the oven," these are, strictly speaking, bite-sized spongecakes coated with pastel-colored, creamy sugar icing. They are served with coffee after—or in place of—dessert.

PHYLLO (GR/ME)

Means "leaf," an apt word to describe this paper-thin sheet of flour-and-water pastry used throughout the Middle East to wrap up sweet and savory fillings in an endless variety of shapes and sizes—from tiny pinwheels, spirals and triangles to large layered casseroles and pies. Some classic phyllo-based pastries includes the BRIK, BAKLAVA and SPANA-KOPITTA. Baked, the phyllo is incomparably crisp and light—qualities akin to those of European strudel dough.

PIBIL (MEX)

A Yucatecan specialty of Mayan origin. Chicken or some other poultry or meat is cut up and marinated for a day in a mixture of citrus juices with garlic, herbs, spices and annatto seeds (*achiote*), the last of which colors the flesh a bright red. Then the pieces are wrapped in banana leaves and baked in a large pot for several hours, until very tender. The leaves are torn away by the diner before he eats the meat. Originally, the dish was cooked in a deep pit—a *pib*, in Mayan.

alla PIÉMONTESE (IT)

Just as Périgord in France is the home of the black TRUFFLE, so the Piedmont region in northern Italy is the home of the white variety. Any dish attributed to the Piedmont is likely to include shavings of white truffle. Sometimes, it will instead feature one of the region's other trademarks: Fontina cheese, anchovies, garlic or rice.

PILAF (ME)

This Turkish rice dish, popular throughout the Middle East, is made by sautéing the grains in butter or oil until they are slightly golden, then simmering them gently in broth with seasonings until they are light and fluffy—the perfect side dish to stews or KE-BABS. Often, a pilaf will become a meal in itself, cooked with scraps of meat and vegetables and garnished with raisins, pine nuts or similar flourishes. Occasionally, burghul (cracked wheat) may replace the rice.

PIPERADE (FR)

Some call this the national dish of the Basques. It is fitting that it should be such an honest, simple dish: chopped peppers, pimientos, tomatoes, onions and garlic are fried in lard or olive oil until very soft. Then beaten eggs are stirred into the mixture until they've barely set. The result is an aromatic omelet, peasant-style, perfect as a luncheon dish.

PIROZHKI (RUS)

The traditional accompaniment to Russian soups such as BORSCH and SHCHI. These finger-sized, crescent-shaped pastries may contain any number of fillings: chopped meat, flaked fish, sautéed onions and cabbage, chopped onion, egg and mushrooms.

PISSALADIÈRE (FR) *or* **PISSALADEIRA** (IT)

As its names might suggest, this specialty of the Riviera and the region of Naples is a forerunner of the familiar pizza. A popular snack or luncheon dish, it is made from a bread dough, flattened into a large rectangle and covered with anchovies, onions, tomatoes, olives, olive oil, herbs and seasonings— and only occasionally cheese. Baked until its edges are browned, it is cut into squares or rectangles and may be eaten hot or cold.

PISTOU (FR)

See PESTO.

PITA (ME)

These small, flat, oval or round yeast breads are quickly baked at a high heat. They puff up, producing pockets at their centers. Perfect for stuffing with such specialities as FELAFEL, HUMMUS and KEBABS, pita are also used as table bread; sliced into fingers and toasted or grilled, they are served to dip in hors d'oeuvres—*mezes*—such as hummus or the Greek TARAMASALATA.

PITHIVIERS (FR)

From the town of the same name comes a two-crust puff-pastry pie, filled with the thick almond-paste buttercream known in France as *frangipane*. The top pastry crust is customarily decorated before baking with spiral incisions and a scalloped edge. Sometimes, in a gentle break from tradition, firm fresh fruits are included in the filling; Pithivier with pears is one exquisite version worth seeking.

alla PIZZAIOLA (IT)

Any pasta, poultry or meat served with a garlicky, herbed tomato sauce that may also include onions, peppers or mushrooms.

POIVRADE (FR)

This pepper sauce is a mixture of finely chopped carrots, onions and celery, sautéed in butter, simmered with wine and stock, and heavily peppered. It is traditionally served with game but may accompany other meats as well.

POJARSKI (RUS/EE)

A Polish innkeeper in czarist Russia created and gave his name to this succulent mixture of chopped veal or chicken, breadcrumbs, cream and seasonings. Shaped into cutlets and coated with more breadcrumbs, pojarskis are pan-fried in butter and oil.

POLENTA (IT)

A porridge of cornmeal. Imperial Romans loved a cereal porridge called *pulmentum,* which they had taken from Etruscan kitchens. They spread it as far as England, where it formed the basis of YORKSHIRE PUDDING. The dish, called polenta today, is still a favorite. Then, it was made with millet, wheat or chick peas; since the seventeenth century, when corn from the New World first became popular in Italy, the ingredient of choice has been cornmeal. Polenta is particularly prevalent in the northern provinces, where it is served as a side dish with roast meats or most typically, with tiny roasted game birds that are eaten whole. The polenta is prepared by cooking it as a porridge, then spreading it on a tray to cool and set; it is then sliced and sautéed in butter until browned. Slices may also be topped with butter and cheese and baked as a GRATIN.

à la POLONAISE (FR)

A Gallic version of a Polish home-style treatment for vegetables such as asparagus and cauliflower. Boiled and drained, the vegetables are placed in a buttered serving dish, sprinkled with chopped egg yolk and topped with breadcrumbs fried in lots of browned butter.

PORCINI

See MUSHROOMS.

PÖRKÖLT (EE)

Like GULYÁS, it is a paprika-flavored stew. It differs from that better-known dish in its higher concentration of paprika and onions; its coarser chunks of meat, which are usually veal or chicken; and its sour-cream gravy.

POT-AU-FEU (FR)

Literally, the "pot in the fire" that always simmered in the rustic hearth year after year, its broth rich with whatever bones, trimmings and aromatic vegetables were available. In restaurants, it is an abundant dish of beef or beef and veal (and in sheep-raising regions lamb or mutton)—a selection of shank, short ribs and rump or top round—poached in good stock and served with onions, carrots, turnips and cabbage that have been cooked briefly in the same liquid.

POTÉE (FR)

Technically, anything prepared in an earthenware pot. Today, however, the term is usually understood to mean a rustic, salt-pork-

and-cabbage soup, with potatoes and other vegetables added as available.

POTTED (UK)

Applies to any meat, game, poultry or fish that is pounded with butter or lard and packed in small earthenware pots (similar to the French RILLETTES). The fat acts as a preservative as well as an enrichment. The potted meat is served with toast or bread as a first course or as a light main course.

POULE-AU-POT (FR)

When King Henry IV proclaimed the ideal of a *poule,* or chicken, in every pot, he had this native dish of Béarn in mind. It is heartwarming food: A hen is stuffed with ham, bread, eggs and chicken liver, all moistened with a little Armagnac. It is then poached in broth with onions, carrots, turnips, leeks and herbs. First the broth is served, followed by plates heaped with the meat and vegetables; as an added garnish, extra stuffing may be wrapped in cabbage leaves and cooked in the pot with the chicken for the last 20 minutes. As with POT-AU-FEU, the best accompaniments are CORNICHONS, coarse salt, bread and a simple red or white wine.

PRAGERSCHINKEN

See HAMS.

à la PRESSE (FR)

''Pressed'' is a treatment applied to duck— particularly to the celebrated ducks of Rouen, which are smothered to death rather than bled, retaining all their blood for a more succulent flesh. The duck is roasted just until its breast meat is done; the legs, still very rare, are then removed and popped under a broiler for further cooking. The breast meat is carved thin and arranged on a heated serving platter in a pool of very concentrated red wine. The carcass of the bird goes into a duck press, like a large vertical vice; the press is cranked and out of its spout emerges a heady extract of the bird's juices. A dash of brandy is added; the sauce is poured over the breast meat; and a few small dabs of butter are placed on top to melt and mingle with the juices. Just before serving, the legs—now done—are added to the platter.

à la **PRINTANIÈRE** (FR)

"In the style of springtime," it could only mean a bounteous garnish of tender new vegetables—peas, string beans, baby carrots, tiny turnips and delicate asparagus tips, all bathed in butter. They may be added to a stew, as in the classic NAVARIN *printanier,* or arranged decoratively around a roasted or braised whole bird or cut of meat.

PROFITEROLES (FR)

Small balls of pastry. Light-textured and hollow within, they are made to be filled with whipped cream or egg-rich pastry cream to make cream puffs (the building blocks of CROQUEMBOUCHE); with ice cream, perfect for a chocolate sauce topping; or with a mousse-like meat or vegetable purée, as an hors d'oeuvre or a garnish for soups.

PROSCIUTTO

See HAMS.

à la **PROVENÇALE** (FR)

Means "in the style of Provence," the Mediterranean province where the sunshine produces voluptuous tomatoes, fecund olive trees, pungent garlic and onions and herbs that perfume the hillsides. Any combination of these ingredients may put the mark of Provence on a dish—be it a sauté or a braise or a stew of meat, poultry or the Mediterranean's splendid seafoods.

PUFFBALL

See MUSHROOMS.

PULCINI

See PASTA.

alla **PUTTANESCA** (IT)

Means "whore style." There is nothing delicate about this Neapolitan spaghetti sauce of tomatoes, garlic, dried red chili, capers, anchovies, black olives, olive oil, oregano, parsley and salt and pepper.

The character of a people can be deduced simply from its way of roasting meat. A beefsteak prepared in Portugal, in France and in England, may give a better clue to the intellectual differences among these peoples than does the study of their literatures.

—EÇA DE QUEIROZ

QUADRICCINI
See PASTA.

QUENELLES (FR)
These dumplings are to the savory world of seafood, poultry and meat what meringues are to the world of confectionery. Their incomparable lightness comes from mixing a purée of the featured ingredient with egg whites, stirring heavy cream into the mixture over ice, then poaching the resulting firm paste—as tiny piped shapes or larger, egglike forms. As they cook, the quenelles puff up, doubling in size. They make an elegant garnish for soups. They may also be served as an hors d'oeuvre or a light main course.

QUESADILLAS (MEX)
Begin with freshly made TORTILLAS flavored with chili, cheese or marrow. They are folded in half around a cheese-and-chili sauce and sometimes meat and beans; then they are crimped shut and deep-fried, to be served as an hors d'oeuvre or a luncheon main course.

QUICHE (FR)

The origin of these delicious dairy-based tarts is disputed. The Germans claim that their *kuchen*, essentially similar in style, are the true ancestors of quiche; the very name in French, they say, derives from the German word. Residents of Alsace and Lorraine also claim the dish as their own, a fact which does not really clarify the national origin of the quiche, since both those regions have been disputed by France and Germany for centuries. Regardless, the true, original quiche recipe is conceded to be that which goes by the name of Quiche Lorraine. The oldest recipes specify thinly rolled bread dough for the crust, though short crust or even puff pastry are substituted today. Thick cream, fresh butter and beaten eggs are mixed together, poured into the crust-lined pan and baked quickly until the filling thickens. Ham, bacon or Gruyère cheese may be added to the mixture before baking, but contrary to popular opinion, cheese is not an essential ingredient of the Quiche Lorraine. In its native regions, the pastry, sometimes spelled *kiche*, is served hot as an hors d'oeuvre. Some dessert tarts nowadays are also called quiche, but they are really just sweetened custard.

QUILLET (FR)

This Parisian cake consists of a rich, butter-and-egg pastry, filled and iced with an equally rich butter cream. The flavoring ingredient is *orgeat*, an almond-flavored syrup.

R

Appetite comes in eating.
—RABELAIS

RACLETTE (SW)

From *racler*, which means "to scrape." It is a melted cheese dish made with a mild cheese from the canton of Valais. A large chunk of the cheese, named raclette after the dish it is chiefly used in, is held in front of a live fire—or a special table-top electric raclette heater—until it just begins to melt. The hot, soft surface of the cheese is scraped onto a warm plate, from which it is eaten with boiled or baked potatoes, pickled onions and CORNICHONS, a hearty, casual feast. The heating, scraping and eating are repeated until every diner has had his fill.

RAGÙ (IT)

Bologna's famous meat-and-tomato sauce for PASTA. Chopped veal and pork, carrots, onions and garlic are gently fried in butter, then simmered for hours with wine, tomatoes and herbs until the mixture reduces to a thick consistency and the flavors to a sublime and heady blend. It is fitting that the word comes

133

from the French *ragoûter* (also the source of a catch-all word for stew, *ragoût),* which means "to restore the appetite."

RAITA (IN)

A yogurt salad. Composed of thick, rich yogurt (in India, made from buffalo milk) with small pieces of cucumber, spinach, tomato, onion or other cooked or raw vegetables, singly or combined, and subtly seasoned with spices such as coriander and cumin. There are even fruit raitas, with banana, grapes, pineapple or other fruits. Served chilled, raitas make a fine foil to fiery curries; they can also be eaten as a light meal with NAAN, CHAPATI, PURI or some other native bread.

RATATOUILLE (FR)

This vegetable stew from Provence combines the heady flavors of the Mediterranean: tomatoes, eggplant, zucchini, onions, peppers, garlic, olive oil and herbs such as oregano and thyme. Garnished with lemon wedges, it may be served hot or cold, as an appetizer or as a side dish.

RAVIGOTE (FR)

The name of this cold sauce for fish or meats comes from the verb *ravigoter,* meaning "to refresh" or "revive." It's a refreshing combination of FINES HERBES, capers, onions, chopped egg and sometimes mustard, mixed into a VINAIGRETTE or into mayonnaise.

RAVIOLI

See PASTA.

RELLENO (MEX)

Means "stuffed," and, technically speaking, it can apply to any dish with a stuffing. In common usage, however, the word usually refers to the *chile relleno.* Large, relatively mild green chilies, particularly the variety known as *poblano,* are roasted, skinned, seeded and stuffed. Fillings may be PICADILLO, chopped chicken, FRIJOLES REFRITOS or other savory combinations, but the most popular choice is a mild cooking cheese such as Monterey Jack. The stuffed peppers are dusted with flour and then dipped in a light egg batter and deep-fried. Finally, the rellenos are put in a casserole, covered with a tomato-and-chili sauce and with more cheese, and baked.

RÉMOULADE (FR)

A *rémouleur* is a knife sharpener; rémoulade is a mayonnaise sauce sharpened with mustard, chopped CORNICHONS, capers, FINES HERBES, scallions and anchovies. It lends a keen edge to the flavor of cold fish.

RIGATONI

See PASTA.

RILLETTES (FR)

A savory country meat spread served as an appetizer on fresh bread or toast. A popular preparation for over 200 years, it is made by simmering small pieces of fat and lean pork, goose or rabbit in seasoned water until all the water evaporates and the meat turns crisp and brown. All the solids are then pounded in a mortar, blended with fat to make a smooth paste and left to cool. The result is seductively rich and savory. Sealed in earthenware pots under a solid layer of fat, the spread keeps well for weeks. Though rillettes are made all over France, those from Le Mans and Tours are the best. See also RILLONS.

RILLONS (FR)

Also called *rillauds* and *rillots*, these are provincial meat preserves akin to RILLETTES. Scraps of pork, goose or rabbit meat are crisped in their own fat; unlike *rillettes*, however, the tidbits are drained, left whole and eaten hot or cold with salt and pepper.

RINDFLEISCHKOCHWURST

See WURSTS.

RISOTTO (IT)

"It seems to be made of grains of gold, each one distinct, each one gilded": so the French gastronome Pomiane described Milan's most famous dish, *risotto alla Milanese*, the classic accompaniment to OSSO BUCO. Plump grains of rice are gently sautéed in butter with minced onion. Then, little by little, a mixture of chicken stock or white wine and water is stirred in, each new addition coming only when the previous one has been absorbed; over the course of an hour's cooking, the rice develops a lovely creamy consistency. The last addition of liquid includes dissolved saffron, the source of the risotto's golden color; before serving, butter and grated Parmesan are stirred in. In other parts of Italy, other kinds of risotto can be found. Some of them are served as main courses: Venice's *risotto di mare* includes mixed seafoods; a Veronese version is made with ham and mushrooms; and in Tuscany a "black" risotto is made with squid and the squid's ink. No matter what their ingredients, though, all risotti will have the same suave character.

RISSOLE (FR)

A meat turnover, made of chopped and seasoned meat wrapped in shortcrust or flaky pastry and deep-fried. Small rissoles may be served as hors d'oeuvres, larger ones as main courses. They originated in the thirteenth century as *roinsolles*, a plain variety of crêpes; only later did they get their meat fillings.

ROBERT (FR)

A seventeenth-century *saucier* named Robert Vinot devised this sauce for grilled pork. He sautéed chopped onion in butter, sprinkled on flour as a thickening agent, added white wine and veal stock and simmered the mixture to coating consistency. The final touch, to offset the sweetness of pork, is a dollop of mustard.

RØDGRØD MED FLØDE (SC)

Literally means "red gruel with cream." It is a popular Scandinavian dessert made of puréed raspberries and currants, thickened with arrowroot and chilled. Individual bowls of the purée are liberally laced with chilled light cream and eaten like a cold fruit soup.

ROES

Ripe fish eggs, or roe, have been appreciated by gourmets at least since the Middle Ages. Although roes may be eaten fresh, most often they are preserved with salt in a simple but painstaking process. The roes are gently pressed through a wide-mesh screen to separate them from each other and from the thin membranes that hold them together. Then the eggs are tossed with fine salt and packed into jars or cans. Many fish have marvelous-tasting roes: the large, orange-pink eggs of the salmon, the grayish eggs of lumpfish, the pinhead-fine eggs of cod (which in Greece are smoked and puréed in the dip called TARAMASALATA). Even the lobster has an excellent roe, called its coral. But the most renowned roe is that of the sturgeon—the only roe that can properly be called by the name "caviar." A century ago the sturgeon, or rather several related species of sturgeon, were widespread in the waters of the northern hemisphere, and caviar was abundant; it was even a frequent offering as a bar snack in the United States and Europe. Pollution and overfishing have severely cut the sturgeon population; with ever-increasing demand, the now scarce roe has skyrocketed in price. The best caviar has a very delicate and not overly salty flavor; its taste should evoke only faint memories of the sea, and those who claim it is fishy have eaten caviar beyond the peak of freshness. The only accompaniment fine caviar needs is thin slices of fresh toast, without butter; champagne or iced vodka are appropriate drinks. Chopped egg, onion and sour cream detract from caviar's flavor, and their secret purpose is to help extend a meager portion of the roe. The best caviar, and the bulk of the world's supplies today, comes from the Baltic and Caspian seas of the Soviet Union and northern Iran. Several names designate the different grades and varieties:

Beluga. The beluga sturgeon produces the largest, most highly prized and priced eggs, ranging in color from black to dark pearly gray.

Golden Caviar. The sterlet, a rare species of sturgeon, has golden-colored roe, an unsurpassed delicacy that was reserved for the czars.

Malossol is not the name of a species of sturgeon but, rather, Russian for "lightly salted." It designates the highest grade of caviar.

Osetrova is a smaller species of sturgeon than the beluga, and its caviar is composed of smaller, darker eggs, still of excellent flavor.

Payasnaya is bricks of pressed caviar, made from more heavily salted, broken or immature osetrova and sevruga eggs.

Sevruga. This smallest sturgeon has the smallest roe, dark gray and with an excellent flavor that some gourmets prefer even to that of beluga.

ROLLATINI (IT)

Italy's answer to PAUPIETTES, OISEAUX SANS TÊTES and any other small rolls of flattened beef or veal. These are likely to be stuffed with prosciutto (see HAMS) and cheese, then browned and braised in stock and wine.

ROLLMOP

See HERRINGS.

alla ROMANA (IT)

The cooking of Italy's capital, Rome, is hard to characterize. "In the style of Rome" could mean that the city's famed ricotta cheese is included—tossed with linguine (see PASTA), for example, or baked as a sweet pudding. Or it could signal a simple butter-and-Parmesan topping for GNOCCHI or fettucine (see PASTA). Some dishes earn the name for being cooked with tomatoes, ham, onions, peppers and garlic—tripe (*trippa*), for example, or chicken (*pollo*). Batter-fried cod fillets (*filetti di baca-*

lao) are Roman style; so are baby artichokes (*carciofi*) baked with wild mint and olive oil. The list of diverse dishes could fill pages: a clear indication that all Italian culinary roads lead eventually to Rome.

ROSSINI (FR)

Gioacchino Rossini, the nineteenth-century composer of such great operas as *Othello*, *The Barber of Seville* and *William Tell*, lived in Paris above the Café Foy; every night he dined downstairs. In his honor, a dish of *tournedos*, thick beef fillet steaks, was created. They are fried in butter, topped with FOIE GRAS and TRUFFLES and placed atop fried bread. Its sauce, a medley of Madeira and beef stock, is simmered in the sauté pan to dissolve the rich deposits left by the steaks.

RÖSTI (SW)

A large, round, crisp brown cake of boiled and shredded potatoes cooked in butter. It is the signature of German-Swiss dining. Originally a breakfast dish, nowadays it is served alongside meats and may be used to soak up stew gravy. Gruyère cheese or diced onion are sometimes added to the potatoes.

à la ROUENNAISE (FR)

An alternative phrase sometimes used to refer to duck cooked *à la* PRESSE, because the ducks traditionally used for the preparation come from Rouen in the northwestern province of Normandy.

ROUILLE (FR)

A fiery sauce of green peppers, dried chilies, garlic, olive oil and water, bound with breadcrumbs. Rouille is served in a sauceboat to accompany the famous fish stew called BOUILLABAISE and some other seafood stews of the French Mediterranean. Each diner seasons his portion to taste with the sauce.

ROULADEN (GE)

Means "rolls." In this case, large pieces of flattened steak are topped with bacon, pickles, herbs, onion and mustard, then rolled, tied and braised. Cut into thick slices, the

139

rouladen are served with braised red cabbage
and potato dumplings.

ROYALE (FR)

A regally rich sauce for poached chicken,
made of a mixture of very thick VELOUTÉ
sauce and puréed TRUFFLES. The name also
applies to plain or flavored custard cut-outs
that garnish many CONSOMMÉS.

RUOTE

See PASTA.

RUSSIAN COOKING

The Soviet Union encompasses many different
cuisines: the Middle Eastern style of cooking in
its southwestern and southern republics; the Oriental tastes of the Mongolian S.S.R.; the marked
Scandinavian flavor detectable in some Estonian
cooking; the Polish and German flavors in the
kitchens of Latvia and Lithuania. But when Russian cuisine is spoken of, what is usually meant is
cooking as practiced in the western, European
part of the Russian republic. The cooking there
has hearty peasant roots, with rich overtones of
Russia's imperial past. There are abundant
spreads of hors d'oeuvres known as *zakuski*;
filling soups like BORSCH and SHCHI with their
toppings of sour cream; elegant main courses like
the pastry-enclosed KULEBIAKA and beef STROGA-
NOFF; and BLINI with their myriad fillings from jam
to caviar (see ROES).

*Intellectuals who wolf down with
a kind of disdain whatever
nourishments their bodies need,
may be very rational and keenly
intelligent—but they are not men
of taste.*
        —SAINTE-BEUVE

SABAYON
> See ZABAGLIONE.

SACHERTORTE (AU)
> A dense chocolate spongecake layered with apricot jam and coated with a thick bittersweet chocolate icing.

à la SAINTE-MENEHOULD (FR)
> Named for a district in the northern province of Champagne famed for pig butchery, this is the classic country treatment for trotters. The pigs' feet are poached in stock and wine until tender, then halved lengthwise, boned, coated with buttered breadcrumbs and mustard and broiled. The same recipe is delicious when used for other homey cuts like breast of lamb or oxtail.

SALAM LEAF (SEA)
> A spicier cousin of the bay leaf. Salam is indispensable to many of Indonesia's aromatic braises.

SALMAGUNDI (UK)
> Old English cookery liberally mixed all kinds

of seemingly incompatible ingredients. Such is the case in this salad of leftover meat or poultry, diced and tossed with onions, hard-boiled eggs, anchovies, beets, pickles and even grapes. *The Joy of Cooking* describes the result as "agreeable anarchy."

SALPICON (FR)

Describes any food finely diced and bound with a hot or cold sauce, as a salad; a side dish; a filling for BARQUETTES, CROÛTES, VOL-AU-VENTS and other edible containers; or as the basis of breadcrumbed and deep-fried croquettes or cutlets. A salpicon of lobster, for example, may be mixed with mayonnaise and served as a main-course luncheon salad; potatoes tossed with the same dressing or a VINAIGRETTE might garnish a plate of cold meats. A chicken salpicon made with a standard BÉCHAMEL could fill a VOL-AU-VENT; if its sauce were cooked to a thicker consistency, the mixture could easily be shaped into croquettes. Salpicons of mixed fresh fruits, doused with a liqueur, make excellent fillings for tarts and other pastries.

SALTIMBOCCA (IT)

The name of this widely loved Roman veal dish promises a taste so delightful it will "jump into the mouth." Pounded scallops of veal are topped with fresh sage leaves and tissue-thin PROSCIUTTO slices, then sautéed in butter and finished with a white-wine sauce. Sometimes cheese—Parmesan, Pecorino or aged provolone—is melted on top.

SAMOSAS (IN)

Small triangular turnovers in a thin, flaky pastry crust, popular as snacks all over India. Vegetarian versions are usually stuffed with spiced potato, sometimes mixed with peas or other vegetables. Otherwise, the filling will be a fairly dry mixture of minced lamb or beef, chilies, herbs and spices.

SASHIMI (JA)

Often merely translated as "raw fish," this is as fair to sashimi, a refreshing appetizer or light luncheon dish, as it would be to call a charcoal-grilled steak "charred flesh." There is nothing distastefully fishy about sashimi, as long as the fish is impeccably fresh—which it will be in a reputable restaurant. Like classic raw-meat dishes—steak TARTARE, CARPACCIO, and KIBBEH—the fish is nicely complemented by sharp seasonings, in this case a dipping mixture of soy sauce and super-hot green WASABI paste, dissolved to taste in the soy; bits of sweet pickled ginger are eaten between bites of fish. Sashimi is prepared to order, each piece quickly and deftly cut to a shape that best suits its taste and texture and the structure of the fish. Favorites are *maguro*, chunks of firm, meaty tuna; *ika*, chewy strips of cuttlefish; *ebi*, whole, soft sweet prawns; *hirame*, thin rectangles of sole; *suzuki*, briny oblongs of striped bass—the choice is wide, and experimentation is encouraged.

SATAY (SEA)

Indonesia's answer to KEBABS is found in great variety throughout the country's 3,000 islands, with each locale offering its own blend of spices. Half-inch chunks of beef, pork, lamb, chicken, shrimp or fish are marinated; threaded on bamboo skewers; and then charcoal-grilled. The sticks of satay are served with a sweet, spicy peanut sauce as well as pieces of cucumber and LONTONG.

SAUERBRATEN (GE)

A sweet-and-sour beef pot roast, the epitome of German country cooking. The sour flavor comes from a vinegary marinade in which the uncooked roast is steeped for several days. Then it is cooked in the marinade with carrots, onions, celery and herbs. To add a sweet edge to the sauce, caramelized sugar is stirred in, often with crumbled gingersnaps; sour cream is an optional addition. To round out a hearty meal, the beef is served with braised red cabbage, stewed apples and potato dumplings.

SAVARIN (FR)

Named in honor of the early-nineteenth-century gastronome and food writer Jean Anthelme Brillat-Savarin, this yeast-leavened cake, similar to a BABA, is baked in a ring-shaped mold (also called a *savarin*) and soaked with a rum or kirsch syrup. Some more elaborate versions fill the cake with CRÈME CHANTILLY or flavor the syrup with cherry juice and place cooked fresh cherries in the ring's center.

SCANDINAVIAN COOKING

What the cooking of these northern countries lacks in sophistication, it more than compensates for with its simple heartiness and abundance: one need look no further than the Danish SMØRREBRØD or the Swedish SMÖRGÅSBORD (or for that matter the related Finnish *voileipäpöytä* and Norwegian *koldt bord*) to see how generous the Scandinavian kitchen can be. Of particular note are the cold fish dishes that start such meals: Bornholmer and Glassblower HERRINGS, for example, or the exquisite Swedish GRAVLAX. Cooked dishes are decidedly homey: dried pea soups; poached fish, roast poultry and game; economical meatballs such as the Danish FRIKADELLER packed with breadcrumbs, egg and seasonings; and simple, satisfying desserts like the puréed berries and cream dish called RODGROD MED FLODE.

SCHLAGOBERS (AU)

Simply sweetened whipped cream, but its ubiquity in Vienna earns it distinguished mention. A crowning glory for any dessert, schlagobers is heaped on cakes, pastries and ice cream; floated in hot coffee or chocolate; or even eaten in a dish on its own.

SCHNITZEL (AU/GE)

See WIENER SCHNITZEL.

SCONES (UK)

Teatime would be a sorry thing without these small, raised breads. A dough of flour, baking powder and buttermilk is rolled out and cut into rounds about 2 to 4 inches across. (Some Scottish scones may instead be 8- to 10-inch rounds, which are served in four wedges.) These are cooked over moderate heat on a lightly greased griddle, until browned on both sides. Split in half, the cakelike scones are buttered and eaten hot, with preserves or a dollop of CLOTTED CREAM. Their name has several possible derivations: the Gaelic *sgonn*, describing the dough's shapeless mass; Low German *schoonbrod*, meaning "fine bread"; or the town of Scone in Scotland.

SCOTCH BROTH (UK)

The name is culinary understatement: no broth could be as unbrothlike as this Scottish lamb stock, chock-a-block with chunks of carrot, turnip, onion, leeks and cabbage, fresh peas and—its most distinctive characteristic—a heap of barley.

SCOTCH EGG (UK)

A favorite pub or picnic food in Britain. Scotch eggs are made by coating peeled hard-boiled eggs with fresh sausage meat and breadcrumbs, then deep-frying them. They may be eaten while still hot but are usually served cold, with mustard or a sweet fruit CHUTNEY, bread and English beer.

SCOTCH WOODCOCK (UK)

In its irony, this is the Scottish equivalent of a Welsh rabbit; like that other British "savoury," this contains no game meat at all. Hot toast is spread with a mixture of mashed anchovies and butter; scrambled eggs are piled on top and decorated with strips of anchovy. Like any savoury, it is served at the end of the meal, after or instead of dessert.

SCRAPPLE (US)

A Pennsylvania-Dutch breakfast dish, it is descriptively named: it is based on scraps of cooked pork, usually leftovers. The meat is mixed with cornmeal and buckwheat and cooked as a sort of thick porridge, which is packed into cake tins and left to set. The resulting loaves are sliced, fried in butter or

bacon fat, and served with eggs in place of—
or alongside—bacon and sausage.

jamón SERRANO

See HAMS.

SEVICHE

See CEVICHE.

SEVRUGA CAVIAR

See ROES.

SHABU SHABU (JA)

The words describe the sound of swishing
water, made by each diner as he prepares his
own serving of this Asian cousin to beef
FONDUE. A seaweed-flavored stock simmers
at table; the guests select from a platter of
thin beef slices, mushrooms, cooked cellophane noodles, Chinese cabbage and spinach,
swishing each morsel in the stock to cook or
warm it, then dipping it in a selection of
sauces—vinegar with DAIKON and scallions,
DASHI with mashed sesame seeds and rice
wine—before eating it. Afterward, the stock,
now well flavored by all the food, is drunk
with rice or noodles.

SHARK'S FIN SOUP (CH)

Reputedly the true test of a Chinese chef's
skill. Dried thin strips of the fin, purchased
ready-prepared from the grocery store, are
soaked overnight to restore their distinctively chewy consistency and subtle marine
flavor. They are then simmered in chicken
broth with shredded chicken breast and Chinese mushrooms (see MUSHROOMS); the soup
is lightly thickened with a touch of corn-
starch. Fine shreds of ham garnish the delicate concoction.

SHASHLIK (RUS)

In the southwestern regions of the Soviet
Union, more truly Middle Eastern than European, this lamb KEBAB—much like the Turkish
shish kebab—is cooked on skewers over an
open fire.

SHCHI (RUS)

Cabbage is the key to this basic vegetable
soup, which may also include carrots, onions,

leeks, celery, turnips, tomato purée and in more abundant versions, beef, sausage or smoked pork. In summer, fresh cabbage is used; winter shchi employs sauerkraut. The soup is usually garnished with KASHA and sour cream.

SHIITAKE

See MUSHROOMS.

SHIRRED EGGS

Eggs are broken into individual, buttered baking cups, then topped with melted butter. The eggs are baked to the desired degree of doneness, then finished with a rich, complementary sauce such as AURORA, SOUBISE or MORNAY.

SHIRUMONO

See JAPANESE COOKING.

SHISH KEBAB

See KEBABS.

alla SICILIANA (IT)

Dishes cooked in the style of the island at the toe of Italy's boot will almost invariably be garnished with Sicily's favorite ingredients: olive oil, garlic, tomatoes, eggplant, anchovies, black olives and capers. The quintessential example is eggplant (*melanzane*) alla Siciliana, stuffed with the other aforementioned ingredients and baked.

SKORDALIA (GR)

A powerful, cold garlic sauce for vegetables, fish or meat. The raw cloves of garlic are smoothly blended with mashed potatoes or fresh breadcrumbs, pine nuts or walnuts, olive oil and vinegar. The sauce enjoys a folk reputation for preventing colds.

SMITHFIELD HAM

See HAMS.

SMÖRGASBORD (SC)

The word is Swedish for "bread and butter table," but that is calling a mountain a molehill. This customary buffet meal, dating from the late nineteenth century, offers dozens of hot and cold dishes on which diners can gorge themselves. To the uninitiated it can be a bewildering array, but a traditional, methodical approach to the meal brings enjoyment and helps avoid indigestion. To begin, a plateful of HERRINGS is in order: briefly marinated, well pickled, smoked, dressed with sour cream and onions, poached, dusted with flour and fried, or however else they may appear. That finished, fill a new plate with other kinds of fish: smoked salmon, jellied eel, GRAVLAX or cod ROE. The third plateful is loaded with cold cuts and salads: such as all manner of HAMS, PÂTÉS and sausages; cold roast beef, pork and chicken; pickled beets and onions; fresh lettuce and tomatoes; sliced cucumber salad; or a MACEDOINE of vegetables in mayonnaise. Finally comes a warmed plate for hot foods: aromatic meatballs of beef, onion and mashed potato (the well-known Swedish meatballs); stuffed onions; fried chicken; meat croquettes; RISSOLES, roast potatoes; and steamed vegetables. Cheese and fruit are likely to follow for dessert. There might also be bread and butter to accompany the meal.

SMØRREBRØD (SC)

These are Danish open-faced sandwiches, with a wide variety of beautifully arranged and garnished toppings—a luncheon tradition for almost 300 years. Thinly sliced, buttered rye, brown or white bread is the foundation (*smørrebrød* means "buttered bread"). Some typical toppings: sliced blue cheese or mellow Tybo with pickled cucumber; cold roast beef with RÉMOULADE sauce; salami with fresh onion rings; smoked salmon with scrambled eggs; poached shrimp on a bed of lettuce, dressed with HOLLANDAISE; pickled herring with fresh apple slices; and cold roast pork with sliced orange and pitted prunes. Beer and aquavit are fitting beverages.

SOPPRESSATA (IT)

In Basilicata, the region at the instep of the Italian boot, this large sausage—a flattened oval in cross section—reigns supreme among preserved meats. It is made of chopped fresh pork, though some towns of the region also include a little smoked ham. The meat is liberally spiced with ginger. Locally, the sausage may be fried and eaten fresh, but if it is intended for travel outside of Basilicata, the soppressata is cured and pressed to its distinctive shape, then preserved in olive oil.

SOUBISE (FR)

Based on puréed boiled onions, this dish takes two forms, both of which accompany roast pork, veal, lamb or chicken, or eggs. Mixed with BÉCHAMEL, it is a sauce; combined with puréed rice for a firmer consistency, it becomes a garnish or side dish.

SOUTHEAST ASIAN COOKING

The gourmet who is familiar with the Chinese and Indian cuisines will find characteristics of both in the kitchens of Southeast Asia. He or she will also find occasional, surprising strains of other, Western cultures—vestiges of the trading nations that plied the seas in this area during past centuries. Last, the gourmet will discover that each nation has some distinct character of its own, making it a cuisine worthy of attention.

Burma. Mild curries, often made slightly sour with tamarind or creamy with coconut, are popular here. Chinese fashion, they are usually accompanied by plain boiled rice. Spiced, vinegared fresh vegetable salads are served as side dishes. Also common are clear soups of fish or pork stock, often embellished with thin egg noodles.

Indonesia. Perhaps the greatest cuisine of the area, and certainly the most varied—with more than 3,000 inhabited islands offering their own versions of the classic dishes. Indonesians use a wonderful palette of flavorings: sweetened soy sauce, sour tamarind, fiery chilies, suave coconut milk, briny shrimp paste, mellow peanuts and tangy ginger plus most of the spices used in the Indian kitchen. Fish, of course, is a key ingredient in this nation of islands; chicken and beef are also very popular; and vegetables are given first-class treatment, cooked with spices or fresh in salads like the simple ACHAR or the grand GADO-GADO; European vegetables like cabbage and cauliflower are frequently used, a legacy of Dutch traders' tastes. The epitome of Indonesian cooking is the Dutch-named *rijsttafel*, or rice table, a buffet comprised of anything from several to dozens of different dishes.

Kampuchea, Laos and Vietnam. Of these three neighboring nations, Vietnam has the most sophisticated and distinctive cuisine, a light, southern Chinese style of cooking lent its own character by liberal use of the fermented shrimp sauce called *nuoc mam;* chilies; and lemon grass, a thin reed with a pronounced lemony tang. All these flavor the country's most famous dish, HANOI SOUP, a main-course soup that is usually served at breakfast in its homeland. The flavorings also contribute much to Kampuchean and Laotian cooking. Rice is the staple in all three cuisines, and seafood predominates.

Malaysia. The cooking here is very similar to Indonesian cooking, with a slightly greater emphasis on southern Indian-style dishes.

The Philippines. Salt (in the guise of fermented fish paste and fish sauce), sour tamarind, garlic, vinegar and soy are the chief seasonings in the nation's dishes. The Spanish influence from colonial days is reflected in the Spanish-named vinegar stew called ADOBO, the national dish. China's sway is seen in the many tossed noodle dishes.

Singapore. This tiny nation serves the key dishes of the Indonesian and Malaysian kitchens, as well as a cuisine known as Straits Chinese—a hybrid of southern Chinese cooking and the spicier styles found in Southeast Asia.

Thailand. Thai curries are flavored with fresh ingredients rather than the dried spices of India, chilies, lemon grass, coriander, garlic, shallots and lime peel combine with salted shrimp paste to give the cooking a light flavor, occasionally fiery. Thai noodle dishes are delightful, a case in point being the festive MEE KROB.

SOUVLAKIA (GR/ME)
Greek lamb kebabs. See KEBABS.

SPANAKOPITTA (GR)
Translates as "spinach pie." A popular hors d'oeuvre, it is made by layering a mixture of chopped spinach, feta cheese and eggs between two layers composed of six or more sheets of PHYLLO pastry. Baked until well browned, the pie is cut into squares or rectangles. It should always be served hot.

SPÄTZLE (GE)
These tiny dumplings, affectionately named "little sparrows," are a staple of southern German cooking, sopping up the rich gravies of the local stews. At their plainest, they are a simple dough of flour, eggs and milk, pinched or snipped into thumbnail-sized pieces and simmered in boiling water. They may also be stuffed, most typically with liver or cheese. The traditional dressing for the dumplings is butter-browned breadcrumbs.

SQUIRREL FISH (CH)
No such fish as the "squirrel" exists.

151

Rather, it is the name given to a special Shanghai-style preparation for a whole fish—usualy sea bass. The fish is cleaned and its head removed but reserved. Then the fish is filleted—the fillets left attached to the tail—and the meat is deeply scored in a criss-cross pattern. The body and head are floured, deep-fried and arranged on a serving platter; a sweet-and-sour sauce with an assortment of lightly cooked vegetables is poured on top. The Chinese believe that the finished dish resembles a squirrel.

STEAK TARTARE
See TARTAR STEAK.

STOLLEN (GE)
A fruit bread given as a gift and served at Christmas throughout the country. Dresden's version enjoys the greatest renown. A sweetened butter-and-egg yeast dough is packed with rum-soaked candied fruits and slivers of almond—making almost as great a volume of solid ingredients as of dough. Shaped into a free-form loaf and baked, the pastry is topped with a snowy sprinkling of confectioners' sugar.

STOVIE (UK)
A Scottish dish of buttered potatoes, sometimes with onions fried in bacon fat or beef dripping. This homey recipe takes its name from the French *etouffée*. The term refers to the method by which the potatoes are cooked—stewed in a closed casserole over low heat, with little or no added liquid.

STRACIATELLE (IT)
This soup, a Roman specialty, is named "little rags," a quaint description of the shreds formed when a mixture of beaten eggs, flour and Parmesan cheese is stirred into simmering chicken or beef broth. Some versions of the soup also include a little semolina as a thickening agent. Egg-drop soup is essentially similar.

STROGANOFF (RUS)
An elegant beef sauté. The chef to Count

Paul Stroganoff, a nineteenth-century Russian gourmet, invented this dish made with thinly sliced prime beef, sautéed with mushrooms and onions in a sauce of sour cream, tomato, beef broth and wine and seasoned with mustard and lemon juice. To soak up the velvety sauce, stroganoff is served over rice or noodles. The dish's popularity has led to offshoots made with veal, pork or turkey.

SUBRICS (FR)

Croquettes without the breadcrumb coating: a mixture of finely diced meat or vegetables, sometimes with grated cheese, is bound together with raw egg and a thick BÉCHAMEL or VELOUTÉ; then it is pan-fried by the spoonful in butter or oil. Depending on their size and their main ingredients, they may be served as hors d'oeuvres, side dishes or a light main course.

SUIMONO

See JAPANESE COOKING.

SUKIYAKI (JA)

A perfect main course for an intimate or informal meal: tissue-thin slices of beef—less often veal, pork or chicken—are sautéed at the table with vegetables, TOFU and cellophane noodles in a sauce of soy, DASHI and rice wine. When the food is done, each diner plucks out the morsels, dips them in raw beaten egg (an authentic but wholly optional touch) and eats them. Sukiyaki is a recent dish in Japan. Beef was introduced there only a century ago, and farmers were the first to prepare it: The name in fact shows its rustic origin, meaning ''spade-roasted.''

SUNOMONO

See JAPANESE COOKING.

SUPPLI AL TELEFONO (IT)

''Telephone wires'' is a whimsical description of this Roman rice croquette. Inside each breadcrumbed ball of leftover RISOTTO are chunks of mozzarella cheese that melt during deep-frying. When the cooked croquette is pulled apart, the cheese stretches in wirelike strings. In its native region, the dish is made with buffalo-milk cheese.

SUSHI (JA)

It is to the East what the sandwich is to the West: a neat, quick, inexpensive, comprehensive meal, though, like a sandwich, it is subject to some delicious (and more expensive) elaborations. Instead of bread, there is rice—a special, cold, sticky mixture called *shari*—seasoned with rice vinegar, sugar and salt. Combined with raw fish (see SASHIMI) or cooked fish, fresh or pickled vegetables, sweetened omelet or the paper-like sheets of dried seaweed known as *nori* (the same seaweed that becomes LAVER BREAD in the West), the rice is molded into compact, beautifully composed morsels. The sushi is dipped by hand or with chopsticks into WASABI-flavored soy sauce, then eaten in one or two bites; parings of pickled ginger (*gari*) add spark as an accompaniment. The simplest sushi are *nigirizushi*. In this variety, the rice is molded into 2-inch oblongs, smeared with *wasabi* and topped with an artfully cut strip of raw fish fillet such as albacore (*shiro*), tuna (*maguro*), abalone (*awabi*) or porgy (*tai*). Some *nigirizushi* use cooked fish instead—grilled eel (*anago*), for example, or boiled prawn (*ebi*). Popular, too, are strips of sweet omelet, bound to the rice by a ribbon of *nori*. *Nori* comes into its own in the variety of sushi known as *makizushi*. A sheet of the dried seaweed is spread with *shari* rice, seasoned with *wasabi*, topped with a filling of fish, pickled or fresh vegetables, rolled into a cylinder and cut into small pieces. *Tekkamaki* has tuna fillet inside; *oshinkomaki*, spears of pickled DAIKON radish; *kappamaki*, raw cucumber. Most impressive is *futomaki*, a large roll containing a selection of six different ingredients that in sliced cross sections forms a beautiful mosaic. Sushi bars, at which diners sit and watch as skilled chefs prepare their food to order, are springing up all over the world; wary Western diners are soon won over by the fresh, clean flavors and the exquisite beauty of the food, not to mention the comparatively reasonable prices. Tea, beer or rice wine (*sake*) go well with sushi.

SWISS COOKING

The border is never far away in this Alpine nation, and the country across the nearest border will largely determine the style of cooking on the Swiss side: French near the west, Italian to the south, German and Austrian to the north and east. Two of the most distinctive native Swiss dishes reflect the country's emphasis on dairy products: the RACLETTE and the cheese FONDUE. Swiss cheese also graces the veal dish dubbed CORDON BLEU, and cream enriches the sauce of the local version of the French veal preparation called ÉMINCÉ. Plenty of butter contributes to the browned crust of the renowned Swiss potato pancake, RÖSTI. A dessert version of the fondue features the premier Swiss confection: creamy milk (or plain) chocolate.

SZECHWAN COOKING

See CHINESE COOKING.

T

He who distinguishes the true savor of his food can never be a glutton; he who does not cannot be otherwise.

—HENRY DAVID THOREAU

TABBOULEH (ME)

This Lebanese salad, popular throughout the Middle East, is based on steamed burghul (cracked wheat). The grain's nutlike flavor is the perfect foil to the other ingredients: chopped tomatoes, onions, scallions, mint, parsley, olive oil and lemon juice. The result is virtually a vegetarian version of KIBBEH.

TACO (MEX)

A fresh corn TORTILLA is folded around a cooked filling: chopped or ground beef or pork or shredded chicken are the usual choices. The filling is dressed with chili sauce, shredded lettuce, tomato, cheese and some sliced avocado or GUACAMOLE. Eaten without further ado, the result is a soft taco. But the taco is more frequently deep-fried to make a crisp version.

TAGLIATELLE

See PASTA.

TAHINI (ME)

The smooth, oily paste that comes from

crushing sesame seeds. It is used as a dressing, a condiment, a dip and a cooking ingredient throughout the region, adding a suave consistency and distinctively nutty flavor to such dishes as puréed eggplant and the chickpea dip called HUMMUS. On its own, tahini is often mixed with lemon juice, garlic, salt and water to make the dip *tahini taratoor*.

TAJINE (ME)

The name of the ubiquitous earthenware casserole of North Africa. Any dish cooked in it takes on the name. Most often, this will be a thick stew of mutton, goat or chicken—even camel—cooked with tomatoes, onions, chick peas and other vegetables.

TAMALES (MEX)

Dating back to Aztec times, their most basic version is made from a simple dough—coarse cornmeal, baking soda and water—that is spread in a rectangle on a corn husk or banana leaf (nowadays, foil or waxed paper may be substituted); folded up in its wrapper to form a neat package about 4 inches long and an inch or two wide; tied up; and then steamed. Unwrapped, the *tamal* (incorrectly known by the singular English "tamale") is eaten as a sort of cornmeal porridge dumpling. But this basic tamal is seldom left unadorned: the recipe invites elaboration with fillings embedded in the cornmeal. The standard filling consists of minced beef, pork, chicken or turkey in a thick sauce of tomatoes, garlic, chilies and onions; some of the sauce, without the meat, may be reserved to dress the cooked and unwrapped tamales. *Tamales dulces,* sweet tamales, are also popular, though less widely known outside the country. Sugar is included in the dough, which may also be enriched with a little lard; the most popular filling is a mixture of almonds and water-plumped raisins.

TANDOORI (IN)

A style of northern Indian cooking, it takes its name from the *tandoor,* a large, curved jar-shaped clay oven, heated by charcoal and usually embedded in the ground. The utensil, introduced throughout Central Asia by the Moguls, simultaneously grills, bakes and roasts. Chicken, seafood or lamb is marinated in yogurt, chilies, spices and saffron or red food-dye for color, then spitted and barbecued in the heat of the *tandoor;* occasional basting with *ghee* (clarified butter) ensures unsurpassed succulence. Indian breads such as ROTI, NAN and CHAPATI can also be baked in the *tandoor:* one end of the uncooked bread is stuck to the upper wall of the oven to hang and cook over the embers.

TAPENADE (FR)

A Provençal condiment and hors d'oeuvre dip that distills all the most pungent flavors of the French Mediterranean. Black olives and salt anchovies are the primary ingredients, puréed with capers, strong olive oil, lemon and a healthy dash of Cognac; other occasional additions are tuna, garlic, oregano and thyme. The paste is served as a dip for crudités or spread on toast.

TARAMASALATA (GR)

Eaten as a *meze*, this dip gets its rosy pink color and briny flavor from the ROE of red *tarama,* or carp in Greek. The roe is blended with fresh breadcrumbs, olive oil, lemon juice, onion and sometimes garlic. Chilled, it is served with fingers of grilled PITA bread.

TATIN (FR)

The family name of two sisters who kept an inn on the road from Paris to Toulouse before World War I. It refers to a caramelized apple tart they invented. The apples are first caramelized in a pan on top of the stove; a shortcrust or puff pastry is placed on top, and the tart is baked; finally it is inverted onto a serving dish. It has become a fashionable dessert, and the term is now evolving to cover similar pies, particularly a fresh pear tart Tatin.

TEMPURA (JA)

Describes any food or combination of food—particularly seafood and vegetables—dipped in an exceptionally light, thin batter and deep-fried. The pieces of food emerge encased in crisp filigree; bite by bite, they are dipped in a sweetened sauce of soy, DASHI, rice wine and grated DAIKON. Popular as tempura is in the West, it is ironic that the dish is actually Portuguese in origin. In the sixteenth century, missionaries to Nagasaki introduced the cooking technique of deep-frying, and the name probably comes from the Portuguese *temporas,* for the Catholic fast days, during which only seafood may be eaten. But the Japanese have since contrived their own explanation of the name: *Tem* means "heaven," *pu,* "woman," and *ra,* "silk"—a metaphor for the delicately coated foods.

TERIYAKI (JA)

A cooking technique, literally glaze-grilling, rather than any one dish. Fish, beef, pork or chicken are marinated in a mixture of soy sauce and rice wine, then grilled and basted with the marinade, developing a glaze.

TERRINE

See PÂTÉ.

THERMIDOR (FR)

When the calendar was renamed during the days of the First Republic, this was the name of the midsummer month. Perhaps the lobster dish given this name was invented at that time, although there is nothing particularly summery about it. A fresh lobster is split lengthwise and roasted briefly; its cooked meat is removed and diced. Then a sauce is prepared from white wine, fish stock, herbs and shallots, combined with a thick BÉCHA-MEL, mustard and fresh butter. The shell halves are lined with this sauce, the lobster meat is added, more sauce goes on top, and Parmesan cheese and melted butter finish the assembly. Briefly reheated to form a GRATIN, the lobster halves are presented at table browned and bubbly.

THOUSAND-YEAR EGGS (CH)

Sometimes called ''hundred-year eggs.'' Either way, it is Chinese poetic license, an exaggeration that should not put diners off from these unusual delicacies. Raw chicken eggs are coated with a lime-rich clay and aged for about two months. The chemicals from the clay are gradually absorbed into the eggs, the insides becoming firm and creamy in texture; the white a pale blue color; and the yolk dark, almost black-green. The flavor is subtle, rich and slightly briny, to be savored in small bites.

TOAD-IN-THE-HOLE (UK)

One can almost imagine a nanny conjuring up this whimsical name to coax her unwilling charge to eat his lunch. Fresh country sausages are fried or broiled, placed in a baking pan with a bit of their fat and submerged in YORKSHIRE PUDDING batter. Baked until the pudding is puffed and golden, the sausages lurk—like toads, perhaps—beneath the pudding's crown. The dish may also be prepared with anything from leftover meats to strips of freshly grilled steak.

TOMALLEY

See ROES.

TORRONE

See NOUGAT.

TORTELLINI

See PASTA.

TORTIGLIONE

See PASTA.

TORTILLA¹ (IB)

This pancake-style omelet comes from Andalusia in southern Spain. Its basis is not so much eggs as potato. A generous quantity of the vegetable is sliced and fried in olive oil, sometimes with onions and garlic. Beaten egg is added, and the omelet cooks until its underside is lightly browned; then it is flipped over and browned on the other side. The thick omelet is cut into wedges and eaten hot or cold as a first course or simple main course. In Madrid, the tortilla is invariably served as part of a TAPAS spread.

TORTILLA² (MEX)

The daily bread of Mexico and some of its Central American neighbors, it is made from an unleavened cornmeal dough, flattened into thin pancakes and cooked on a griddle. Today, tortillas are easily mass-produced: Most home kitchens are equipped with cast-iron tortilla presses. Still, many native women continue to practice the art of patting the dough into shape back and forth between their hands. Tortillas may be eaten hot, on the side, playing the same role as bread, but no other bread has so many other culinary uses. Tortillas may be cut into wedges and deep-fried to make chips for dipping GUACAMOLE. They become the containers for such variously shaped and filled main-course creations as TACOS, CHALUPAS, ENCHILADAS, FLAUTAS and TOSTADAS. Stale tortillas are transformed into the satisfying casserole called CHILAQUILES. Crumbled, they are even used to thicken stews such as the Mexican national dish, MOLE *poblano de guajalote*.

TOSTADA (MEX)

If TACOS are akin to standard sandwiches, these are their open-faced counterparts. A large corn TORTILLA is deep-fried, flat, until crisp. Then it is slathered with FRIJOLES REFRITOS; topped with cooked beef, pork or chicken and chili sauce; and garnished with shredded lettuce, tomato, avocado or GUACAMOLE and sour cream. Like the more substantial of the open-faced sandwiches, it is eaten most safely with knife and fork.

TREE EAR FUNGUS

See MUSHROOMS.

TRENETE

See PASTA.

TRIFLE (UK)

A modest name for a luxurious dessert made with sliced spongecake that has been soaked with Sherry, coated with jam and layered in a bowl with sliced fresh or poached fruits, custard and whipped cream. Candied fruits and nuts add a decorative touch. The same dessert is popular in Italy, where it is known as *zuppa Inglese,* or English soup.

TRUFFLES

These are to the world of MUSHROOMS what diamonds are to the world of gems. Indeed, these fungoid treasures, unlike mushrooms, lie hidden beneath the earth—usually around the bases of oaks and other trees. To this day, there have been no successful attempts to cultivate truffles commercially, which explains their extremely elevated price. The truffle hunter must seek them out in an unusual way. Once, it is said, the best truffle hunters were virgin girls. Today, the mundane hunter uses a pig (or, less often, a mongrel dog) who is specially trained to detect and home in on the scent of the precious truffle. Once the animal begins to dig at a certain spot, it is pulled away and its master completes the truffle's unearthing. Although many varieties of truffle exist around the world, only two truly great ones merit culinary consideration: the black truffle found in the Perigord region of central France and the white truffle of the Piedmont in northern Italy.

Black truffles may range in size from that of a small peanut to something approaching a hefty orange, though the most common specimens are about as big as golf balls. They have very knobbly surfaces that need arduous scrubbing to rid them of earth. The truffle is fairly firm, almost crisp in texture, and its brownish-black flesh has a fine, cream-colored marbling. To describe the black truffle's flavor is another matter: adjectives ranging from licoricelike to musky to bosky have been tried. It is a dark, elusive, almost sexual kind of savor (indeed, aphrodisiac powers have been ascribed to them for centuries), a flavor that suffuses any dish prepared with truffles and lingers in the memory. For those with the money to do so, black truffles are best enjoyed whole: braised in Champagne and butter; cooked *sous les cendres*, that is, seasoned, wrapped in bacon, doused with brandy, enclosed in heatproof paper and buried in embers to bake; or *en chaussons*, wrapped in bacon and enclosed in puff pastry to bake as a turnover. Truffles may be sliced and cooked in a cream sauce, stirred into scrambled eggs or fried as fritters, cut into a JULIENNE and served as a salad or puréed with a BÉARNAISE sauce. But because of its price, a small amount of truffle is usually allowed to go a long way in cookery: combined with FOIE GRAS in a PÂTÉ, thinly sliced as a garnish for some elegant sauté or finely minced to perfume a poultry stuffing or a fine homemade sausage. Truffles, in fact, don't even have to be eaten to do their work: if a whole truffle is left in a basket of raw eggs, the eggs will absorb its aroma through their shells, and a truffleless "truffled" omelet can be enjoyed.

White truffles are off-white in color; shaped like small potatoes; and have a flavor, variously described as peppery or garlicky, that is stronger than the black variety. For this it is prized by its devotees; but aficionados of the black variety think this lack of subtlety makes the white inferior. It is better not to bother comparing them and to enjoy the white truffle for its own merits. As a rule, it is used raw, cut into thin shavings that add their perfume to a dish just before it is served: the two classic Piedmontese dishes, FONDUTA and BAGNA CAUDA, both employ the truffle in this way, as do various examples of RISOTTO and omelets. White truffles are also eaten as a salad dressed with olive oil and lemon. They may on occasion be cooked whole or sliced like the black-truffle dishes described above.

TSIMMES (JE)

A sweet-sour side dish of mixed vegetables and fruits, served with roast meat or poultry. The best-known version is carrot tsimmes, which usually combines the vegetable with dried apricots. The name has a simple etymology: The German words *zum*, meaning "to the"; and *essen*, meaning "eating." But the dish itself, mixed-up concoction that it is, has given its name in turn to Yiddish slang: any messy situation or bother is a "tsimmes."

TSUKEMONO

See JAPANESE COOKING.

TURBAN (FR)

A shallow, circular mold with a hole at its center—its shape reminiscent of a Middle Eastern headdress—may be given this name. Any dish based on finely chopped or puréed meat, poultry or fish prepared in such a mold may also be called a "turban": the finest example is a fish turban, the mold lined with fillets of, say, salmon and sole, the inside filled with a light fish MOUSSELINE. Unmolded after baking, the turban is served in wedges with an AURORA sauce or some other flavorful, creamy concoction.

TURRÓN

See NOUGAT.

TZATZIKI (GR)

Yogurt and finely sliced cucumbers are folded together in this cool summer salad, a relative of Indian RAITA. Extra spark comes from fresh mint, scallions and, on occasion, more than a little raw garlic.

Let us give thanks before we turn
To other things of less concern
For all the poetry of the table.
                    —LOUIS UNTERMEYER

UDON (JA)

Thin, flat wheat noodles, the main ingredient of a luncheon main-course soup that also bears the name. Cooked in DASHI, a mass of noodles is garnished with scallions; radish; and in more substantial versions, perhaps small pieces of pork, chicken or seafood or a few pieces of TEMPURA.

UKHA (RUS)

Russian peasants simmer a mixed catch of firm-fleshed white fish in a basic *court bouillon* and serve the resulting clear broth with its chunks of fish. A restaurant might garnish ukha with sliced lime and fresh dill.

UNITED STATES COOKING

America has been called a "melting pot," where immigrants of different nationalities retained their cultural characters and yet blended together to become a single people. It is an apt choice of metaphor. Dining in the United States demands a knowledge of all the world's cuisines:

165

New England is where American cooking began, with the Pilgrim settlers applying good, simple English-style methods to strange new ingredients. They stuffed and roasted turkeys; puréed pumpkins and made them into pies; and cooked the Indian's corn—boiled or roasted whole. They also used the corn dried, ground into cornmeal and transformed into breads and maple-syrup-flavored INDIAN PUDDING. Other immigrants brought still other cooking habits: the French, for example, transformed their native BOUILLABAISE into New England's version of clam CHOWDER.

Mid-Atlantic States. The marvelous seafood includes crab, served heartwarmingly in the form of Maryland's pan-fried crab cakes; clams and oysters, too, exist in great variety. One unique local style of cooking is that of the Pennsylvania Dutch, actually descendants of German and Swiss immigrants. They prepare a sturdy, peasant-style fare exemplified by such dishes as wood-smoked hams, deep-dish chicken pies, SCRAPPLE and SHOOFLY PIE.

The South and New Orleans. Fried chicken, cornbread, HUSH PUPPIES, black-eyed peas, biscuits 'n gravy and hominy grits are just a few examples of the South's down-home style of cooking. Louisiana's premier city, New Orleans, is the home of Creole and Cajun cooking, a spectacular blend of French, English, Spanish, Indian and African influences that has resulted in such heavenly dishes as GUMBO and JAMBALAYA.

Southwest and Tex-Mex. This is a region that celebrates outdoor cooking, where barbecues recall the open pit and campfire cookery practiced by cowboys and early settlers. Of special note is Tex-Mex cooking, that is, MEXICAN COOKING with a north-of-the-border twist: not just chili and beans but a still-developing cuisine that tends to hold back on the spices, only slightly, while compensating with oversized and elaborated versions of Mexican classics like ENCHILADAS, TACOS, and a casserole called *chili con queso* that closely resembles CHILAQUILES.

There is no treasure quite like living at one's ease.

—FRANÇOIS VILLON

alla VALDOSTANA (IT)

The Valle d'Aosta is a French-speaking region in the Italian Alps. Their style of cooking veal chops or chicken breasts involves stuffing them with the Fontina cheese of the nearby Piedmont region, coating them with egg and breadcrumbs, and pan-frying them in butter. On occasion, prosciutto (see HAMS) or shavings of the famed Piedmontese white TRUFFLE will be added to the stuffing.

VELOUTÉ (FR)

Means "velvety," the perfect description for two related classic preparations—a sauce and a kind of soup. Both are made by thickening broth—usually of chicken, veal or fish—with *roux*, a lightly cooked mixture of flour and butter. Velouté sauce adds body to braises such as fricassées and is the basis of such sauces as ALLEMANDE. It is combined with puréed vegetables such as mushrooms, artichokes or celery; puréed seafood such as lobster, crayfish or oysters; or puréed meat

167

or poultry. The sauce is then enriched with cream and egg yolks, and it becomes a thick, smooth soup.

VERMICELLI

See PASTA.

VÉRONIQUE (FR)

Some long-forgotten woman named Veronica was honored with this garnish of white grapes, most often gracing poached fillets of sole in a white-wine-and-cream sauce.

VICHYSSOISE (FR/US)

Classy though its name and reputation may be, this is nothing but a humble French pu-réed leek and potato soup, combined with cream, chilled and topped with chives. It was invented by the late Louis Diat, chef at the Ritz-Carlton Hotel in New York, who named it after his home town, Vichy, and made it chic at the time when he placed it on the Ritz's menu.

VINDALOO (IN)

A fiery curry from the south and west of the subcontinent. Meat or poultry marinates with hot mustard seeds and other spices, garlic and vinegar; then it is cooked in pungent mustard oil with tamarind, onions, more spices and the marinade. The resulting curry is at once searingly hot and puckeringly sour (thanks to the vinegar and tamarind). A RAITA served alongside will help to moderate the curry's heat.

VITELLO TONNATO (IT)

An incomparable and surprisingly subtle pair-ing of meat and fish, one of the world's great cold dishes, served as an appetizer or a main course. The dish begins with a top quality roast of veal (*vitello*). In the fanciest versions, this is pierced with skewers, which are then withdrawn and their holes stuffed with baby carrots; gherkins; and other firm, colorful vegetables. The veal is poached in chicken stock or veal stock flavored with aromatic vegetables and herbs, then left to cool in the liquid. Meanwhile, the sauce is prepared from oil-packed tuna (*tonno*), olive oil, anchovies, lemon juice, capers, cream, and some of the poaching stock—a suave, slightly sharp concoction. Both the veal and the sauce are chilled. Before serving, the veal is sliced—revealing the decorative and colorful pattern of vegetables stuffed through it. The slices are placed on a serving platter, and the sauce is spooned over them, its mellow, tangy flavor perfectly complementing the savor of the veal.

VOL-AU-VENT (FR)

"Flight in the wind" evokes the lightness of these round cases shaped from puff pastry and ranging in size from 1-inch mouthfuls for canapés to larger single-serving or multiple-serving cases several inches across. They may be filled with any mixture of chopped or diced meats, poultry, seafood or vegetables, bound together with a thick sauce such as BÉCHAMEL. Mushroom vol-au-vents are a popular hors d'oeuvre; a chicken vol-au-vent is standard luncheon fare—chicken *à la* KING being the best-known example.

*One cannot think well, love well,
sleep well, if one has not dined well.*
—VIRGINIA WOOLF

à la WALEWSKA (FR)

Countess Marie Walewska was mistress to Napoleon. She is immortalized in this presentation of poached fillets of sole. The cooked fish is garnished with slices of poached lobster and fresh black TRUFFLE, then blanketed with a MORNAY sauce flavored with the lobster's coral (see ROES). The dish is briefly popped under the broiler until the sauce is browned and bubbly.

WASABI (JA)

That cool-looking little mound of bright green paste beside a serving of SUSHI or SASHIMI is deceptive: Wasabi, made from the powdered, dried root of a Japanese horseradish, is hot enough to take away the breath of the unwary. Use only a little.

WATERZOOTJE (BNL)

Water is the starting point of this classic Flemish main-course soup of chicken or fish. A chicken is poached in water with aromatic vegetables; its meat is then cut up and served in the broth, which is enriched with egg yolks and cream. For a fish waterzootje, several varieties of seafood—and always eel—are cut into chunks and simmered with vegetables in water, fish stock and white wine generously enriched with butter. The finished soup is often thickened with crumbled rusks.

WESTPHALIAN HAM
See HAMS.

WIENER SCHNITZEL (AU)
A schnitzel is any thin slice of meat—beef, veal, pork or chicken—cooked in any number of ways. This is its most famous version—Viennese style. Pork or beef may be used, but the classic choice is veal—a slice pounded to tissue thinness, about as big as a dinner plate. The meat is coated with flour, egg and toasted breadcrumbs, then fried in hot lard or lard and butter until the coating is golden. The schnitzel is drained on a kitchen towel—tradition jokingly has it that you should be able to sit on a good schnitzel without staining your trousers—and served at once with lemon wedges to squeeze on top.

WURSTS
Germany's sausages, or wursts, are in a class by themselves. No other country produces such a variety of sausages: sausages cured and eaten raw in slices; sausages smoked, boiled and eaten whole; sausages raw, for grilling or pan-frying. To the uninitiated, the variety of wursts can cause bewilderment; they can be, as a turn-of-the-century phrase put it, "little bags of mystery." With scores of wursts to choose from, there will always be some confusion; even a native-born German cannot hope to know them all. The following list should begin to help dispel the mystery:

Berlinerwurst. Berlin sausage. A smoked and precooked mixture of unseasoned, coarsely ground cured pork and finely minced beef. Eaten cold, sliced.

Bierwurst. Coarse-textured pork with juniper,

cardamom and garlic. Precooked and eaten cold, sliced. In times past it was marinated in beer—hence, the name.

Blutwurst. Blood sausage. Chopped pork and pork fat, mixed with blood, herbs and sometimes gelatine. Precooked and eaten cold, sliced.

Bockwurst. A kind of large Frankfurter. Mostly veal, with a little pork, mixed with milk, egg and herbs. Boiled and eaten whole.

Bratwurst. A frying sausage of finely minced pork or veal, light in color. Sometimes mildly smoked.

Braunschweiger. See Leberwurst.

Frankfurterwurst. The "hot dog." Lean beef and pork, finely minced, mildly seasoned and lightly smoked; the pink color comes from saltpeter. Eaten whole, boiled or grilled.

Knackwurst. A plump sausage made with a filling similar to that of the frankfurter, made slightly spicier with cumin and garlic. Boiled or grilled.

Leberwurst. Liver sausage, always precooked and served cold, usually of spreadable consistency. The common Braunschweiger variety is made from pork and pork liver and is usually smoked; sometimes whole pistachio nuts or chopped TRUFFLE are added. Truffled goose liver is used for an elegant *Gänsleberwurst*.

Mettwurst. A peppery mixture of minced beef and pork, boiled before eating.

Nurnbergerwurst. Nuremberg sausage. Lean pork, bacon fat, herbs, seasonings and a dash of kirsch. Pan-fried in butter.

Rindfleischkochwurst. Finely minced lean beef with pork fat, coriander and seasonings, air-dried for two days. Boiled before eating.

Wienerwurst. Vienna sausage, Austria's frankfurter. Pork with beef or veal, finely minced and lightly seasoned, cured and smoked. Boiled or grilled before eating.

XYZ

Flavors must be rich and robust, never oily, or they must be delicate and fresh without being too thin.

—YUAN MEI

XAVIER (FR)

This soup or *potage* is intensely rich and thick, a cream of rice soup (made with chicken or veal stock) combined with egg yolks, cream and butter, then garnished with chicken-flavored ROYALE dice. It was the creation of Louis Stanislas Xavier, Count of Provence, the future King Louis XVIII.

au XÉRÈS (FR)

Refers to the Spanish town of Jerez, the home of Sherry (itself an English corruption of the town's name). Any dish so labeled will in all likelihood have a sauce flavored with that famous fortified wine.

YAKIMONO

See JAPANESE COOKING.

YAKITORI (JA)

Best known of the category of grilled dishes called *yakimono* (see JAPANESE COOKING), these are grilled chicken KEBABS. Small cubes of boneless chicken meat (and sometimes chicken livers) are cooked on skewers over charcoal and basted with *yakitori* sauce—a mixture of *sake* (rice wine); *mirin* (sweet *sake*); sugar, dark soy sauce; and a thick, sweet soy sauce called *tamari*—which gives the chicken a dark, sweet-and-savory glaze.

YORK HAM
See HAMS.

YORKSHIRE PUDDING (UK)
A traditional accompaniment to English roast beef, it is made by adding a batter of flour, eggs and milk to the hot drippings in the roasting pan, then baking it until puffed and golden-brown. Sections of the sheet of pudding are served with the sliced beef. Made with butter, a Yorkshire pudding may also be served with jam for an informal dessert, somewhat like a popover. Poured over roasted sausages and baked, the pudding becomes a favorite country dish called TOAD IN THE HOLE.

ZABAGLIONE *or* ZABAIONE (IT)
Known in France as *sabayon,* it is an unusual but classic dessert, a frothy custard of eggs and wine. Egg yolks, sugar and Marsala wine are whisked vigorously over gentle heat until they mount to a thick foam; often, this is done at the table, an impressive flourish to end a meal. The light but rich sweet is usually eaten hot, but it may also be chilled before serving. Other sweet or fortified wines, liqueurs, or citrus zest may be included for variety.

ZAMPONE (IT)
An unusual variation on fresh sausage, from the northern town of Modena. Its casing is a pig's trotter, boned and stuffed with a spicy ground-pork mixture. Simmered for several hours, the zampone is sliced and served with other boiled meats and vegetables.

ZARZUELA (IB)
The name of Spain's national operetta, a light, giddy entertainment that, carefully di-

rected though it is, has an air of merry mayhem. No wonder the name has been extended to a fish and shellfish stew that bubbles over with any seafood the market has to offer—crayfish, mussels, prawns, squid, sole, hake, lobster, scallops, clams. Contributing to the gaiety are tomatoes, garlic, peppers, onions, saffron and white wine.

ZINGARA (FR)

The Italian word for gypsy has been adopted to describe this garnish for sautées of poultry or meat. An elegant mixture of shredded ham, tongue, mushrooms and TRUFFLES in a tomato- and tarragon-flavored reduction of beef or veal stock, it is hardly representative of gypsy cooking. Perhaps its bright colors are thought to suggest the gypsy's motley.

ZUPPA INGLESE (IT)

See TRIFLE.